ACCOUNTABILITY

THE

SANDLER
WAY

D0106881

Praise for Hamish Knox's
ACCOUNTABILITY
THE SANDLER WAY

"Contrary to popular belief, accountability is not a dirty word. If you think your sales team, or any part of it, isn't yet ready for an accountability program that features real-world consequences, then Hamish Knox wrote this book for you."
— **Scott Clark,** Corporate Leadership Coach,
Awesome Journey Inc.

"An easy way to integrate accountability — first for yourself, and then for your team. Highly recommended!"
— **Andrew Lozier,** Vice President of Sales, Bulletproof Infotech

"Many sales managers in the energy services sector feel the cost of sales is far too high. Hamish Knox's straightforward approach to adopting an accountability model is an absolute winning formula to solving this problem and building your business."
— **Kevin D. Turko,** CEO, Leadstone Group Inc.

"The perfect book for all those looking to implement an accountability plan within their team — or within themselves."
— **Lindsay Harle,** Owner/Content Consultant, The Write Harle

"Some business books speak generally about big concepts. What differentiates this book is that it gives you both the roadmap and all the practical tools necessary to implement the big concepts, if you so choose. 'Accountability the Sandler Way' can make you much better personally and professionally."
— **Tracie Reed,** Vice President of Sales and
Marketing, Drillform Technical Services Ltd.

ACCOUNTABILITY
——— T H E ———
SANDLER WAY

*Creating a Leadership Mentality
in 20 Minutes a Week*

HAMISH KNOX

ACCOUNTABILITY THE SANDLER WAY
Creating a Leadership Mentality in 20 Minutes a Week

ISBN: 978-0-9832614-9-0

Visit us at www.sandler.com to learn more!

To my wife, Kim, and my daughter, Taylor, who are the reason I go to bed and wake up smiling every day. To my parents, Astrida and Jim, who instilled in me a love for words, and who gave me the freedom to use them. To my mentor and friend, Gordon Griffiths, who introduced me to the wonderful Sandler family. And to my teacher and friend, KruYai Scott Clark, who makes me a better person and martial artist every time we work together.

TABLE OF CONTENTS

FOREWORD

Leading a sales team effectively is a special challenge, one that does not come as easily or as instinctively as we may imagine. Why? Because some great salespeople are not yet great leaders or managers. We may assume that great performance in one specific role — selling — means that a particular person is "cut out" for leading a sales team. That just isn't always the case.

Too many sales teams suffer from what might be called "Superstar Syndrome": a highly productive salesperson is suddenly promoted to management, on the theory that the skills and capacities that lead to personal success in the field of sales are more or less identical to the skills and capacities that lead to success in training and motivating others to sell. They aren't. The team suffers.

In other cases, a manager who has achieved good results in some other area of the enterprise — operations, say — takes over responsibility for "overseeing sales," usually in addition to the responsibility of "overseeing" some other part of the company at the same time. The potential for diverse varieties of disaster in such a scenario is vast, and includes disengagement, micromanagement, personality conflicts, and the ever-popular "I'm telling on you" school of interpersonal communication, which, when appealed to by managers, tends to yield indifferent results at best. Again, the team suffers.

A third distinctive challenge arises when a leader has ample experience in managing a sales team, but has only learned to do so by means of an extensive, time-intensive "mentoring" relationship that works well for a team consisting of two or three people, but can't be scaled up to accommodate a team of fifteen. Once more, the team suffers.

What is the best response to such challenges, which can literally destroy a business? Hamish Knox's new book puts forward a simple one-word answer — Accountability — and proposes, intriguingly, that the key to getting others in the enterprise to apply it to the sales process is to apply it, visibly, in one's own life, and specifically in one's interactions with the members of the sales team. This is one of those "common-sense" ideas that most everyone is likely to agree with, but few managers are prepared to implement on a practical level.

This book turns "common sense" ideas about accountability into a real-world workplace culture of accountability for sales teams and those tasked with leading them. It is rooted in the core Sandler® principles. It should be required reading for everyone responsible for or managing salespeople.

- Shia Fishman
  Sandler Training

INTRODUCTION

For most people, "accountability" is a terrifying word. It usually conjures up images of micromanagers controlling their employees' every move. For an athlete, the word may even trigger memories of doing punishment laps or push-ups, or, in general, we may recall hated chores we had to perform because we failed to live up to someone's ambiguous standard.

Sandler clients discover that repeatable, sustainable success in the world of sales comes from being *accountable* to specific, measureable actions. For them, "accountability" means something very different than what it means for others. It means freedom.

In this book, "accountability" means creating clarity for yourself and your employees around goals (yours and theirs), the path to achieve those goals (yours and theirs), and the consequences triggered by failing to stick to that path. Don't get nervous; no one's going to have to do any punishment laps.

In my experience, chief executives, business owners, sales managers, and other leaders responsible for the performance of sales teams tend to avoid implementing accountability programs for one simple reason. To them, the task of creating the cultural change necessary to make accountability a daily reality feels a little bit like attempting to eat an elephant in one sitting. The job seems impossible.

Fortunately, it's not. The purpose of this book is to help you, the leader of your sales team, eat that accountability elephant one bite at a time.

A warning is in order: As you go through this book, you may get uncomfortable as you reflect on your own skill set and where you might be personally lacking in accountability. Those feelings are perfectly OK. When you reach a challenging section, keep an open mind and journal about your thoughts and feelings around that section. My clients share with me often that journaling in this way helps them internalize and customize Sandler concepts to their world.

Let me share the two keys to successful implementation of an accountability program: trust and communication. If there is no trust between you, the leader, and your employees, your accountability program will fail because your employees will feel you are implementing a program to punish them. If communication about your reasons for implementing a program are unclear, both you and your employees will quickly grow frustrated, and mistrust will develop. As you progress through each chapter make notes on how you can bring clarity to your communication about your accountability program and how you can improve the level of trust between you and the salespeople you lead.

Each chapter of this book features exercises that will help you create the foundation for a successful accountability program. These exercises will help you to build up your own accountability muscles and create an ongoing maintenance plan so your accountability program becomes ingrained in the culture of your organization. You will want to return to this book as your organization changes to go through the exercises again with a different perspective. Because some of the exercises in the book are personal in nature, I suggest you complete the exercises in a separate notebook.

If you are eager to implement a sustainable accountability program for yourself and your team, I wrote this book for you.

Let's get started!

CHAPTER ONE

Myths and Misconceptions about Accountability

Accountability is doing what you agree to do. This sounds simple enough, but most workplace cultures do not support accountability. Before we dive into the details of setting up an accountability program that can transform the working culture, we must deal with the myths and misconceptions about accountability that typically sabotage these programs.

In this chapter, we'll look at four of the top myths and misconceptions about accountability: the "Big Brother" myth (aka the "Micromanager" myth), the "Too Much Time" myth, the "Veteran Team" myth and the "They'll Leave" myth. Once you learn to recognize these four myths, you will be in a much better position to defend your accountability program when one or more of the myths present themselves ... which will happen.

The "Big Brother" Myth

Also known as the "Micromanager" myth, the "Big Brother" myth sits on two cracked pillars.

Pillar one is a manager's need to be liked by employees. What managers sometimes forget is that management is not a place to get their needs met. It is a place to grow their employees.

Pillar two is the common claim from employees that satisfying the demands of "Big Brother's" accountability program somehow prevents them from being productive.

The "Big Brother" myth is the myth that is most likely to undermine or destroy any accountability program. In practice, it often sounds like this: "Don't you trust us?" Let's look at each pillar of this potentially devastating myth in detail.

Pillar One – The Need for Approval

A high need for approval in a manager usually manifests behaviorally as being too permissive with the team — by, for instance, accepting late arrivals to meetings or bending the rules for a "special" situation, which occurs enough for "special" to become "common." The need for approval may also present itself in the form of spending too much time "checking the pulse" or "getting feedback" from the team on decisions that you, as a leader, should make (e.g., standing agenda items for weekly meetings). Each situation is problematic.

Case in Point – Too Permissive

Aidan, Stephanie's manager, implemented an accountability program 4 weeks ago which included weekly individual meetings with each member of his team on Monday for 5 minutes and Friday for 15 minutes. Stephanie has missed the last 2 Monday meetings and the last 3 consecutive Friday meetings. The Monday meetings were only made up when Aidan sought her out on Tuesday; she missed the Friday meetings because of "client emergencies." Here's what Aidan's most recent discussion with Stephanie sounded like.

Aidan: Stephanie, I'm curious about what's causing you to miss our meetings on Monday and Friday.

Stephanie: Oh, I didn't think it was a big deal. I made all my calls and meetings the last three weeks.

Aidan: Well, it's not a "big deal," especially if you're making the number of calls and meetings you committed to, but those meetings are also your opportunity to ask for help or let me know about any small issues that we can fix before they become major issues.

Stephanie: Aww, it's nice of you to say that, but I really don't need a big brother watching my every move. If there's something I can't handle, I'll definitely ask for your help.

Aidan: OK, so I won't have to track you down on Monday or Friday for our meetings anymore?

Stephanie: Unless something with a client comes up.

Aiden: That makes sense. I look forward to our meeting on Friday.

The first problem with Aidan's attempt to defend the accountability program arises when he concedes that Stephanie missing meetings isn't a "big deal." If you want to implement a successful accountability program, regular check-in meetings must be non-negotiable for you and your direct reports. Aidan compounds this problem by allowing Stephanie to create an "out" that makes the meetings optional for her. She says she'll be there "unless something with a client comes up." He agrees to this! Why? Because he requires her approval.

The second problem arises when Aidan appears to give Stephanie tacit permission to avoid accountability ... as long as she makes the required number of calls and meetings each week. Aidan thereby misses a twice-weekly opportunity to identify "yellow flags" — warning signs — in Stephanie's numbers. For example, if she consistently converts only 10 percent of her calls to first meetings when the rest of Aidan's team consistently converts 30 percent of their calls to first meetings, that should be a point of discussion in the Monday and Friday meetings. If Aidan were able to spot these signals, he could coach her while tracking her progress in subsequent weeks. But because he requires Stephanie's approval, he has given up this twice-weekly warning system.

The third and perhaps biggest potential problem Aidan creates here is allowing Stephanie to determine what is a big enough issue with a client to bring to him. She informs him that she'll be in touch if there's something she can't handle. He accepts that, again because Stephanie's approval is important to him.

This is a problem because salespeople typically don't bring something to their manager's attention until the issue is the equivalent of an out-of-control forest fire! What we'd prefer is that they bring us the issue when it's still a small campfire that can be easily controlled.

In addition, by allowing Stephanie to skip her weekly meetings, Aidan puts himself in a position to fall victim to the "Too Much Time" myth, which we'll cover later in this chapter.

Let's look at how that conversation might go if Aidan didn't have such a high need for Stephanie's approval.

Aidan: Stephanie, I'm curious about what's causing you to miss our meetings on Monday and Friday.

Stephanie: Oh, I didn't think it was a big deal. I made all my calls and meetings the last three weeks.

Aidan: I'm glad you hit your cookbook* targets, but do you remember what I said to the team when we rolled out this program?

Stephanie: Yeah, that these "check-in" meetings were non-negotiable. I just don't get why we need them. I don't need to be micromanaged!

Aidan: Thanks for sharing, Stephanie. Help me understand what you mean by "micromanaged."

Stephanie: Aidan, I'm totally committed to this program. In fact I like how my cookbook shows me how I'm progressing toward my goals, but sitting down with you at 2 p.m. every Friday makes me feel like I'm being sent to the Principal's office each week.

Aidan: OK, I'm starting to understand now. I'm curious: why do you believe we have these meetings?

Stephanie: I don't know.

Aidan: (Pauses for ten seconds.)

Stephanie: If I had to guess, it's time you set aside in your calendar just for me in case there's an issue with which I need help.

Aidan: You're spot on. Tell me, do you feel like we have to meet for the entire time we set aside?

Stephanie: Well that's kind of how meetings go, right? If I

---

* "Cookbook" is Sandler's word for a behavior plan. In sales, a cookbook defines the specific prospecting and account management activities and the amount of each activity a salesperson would complete on a monthly basis. For example: number of prospecting calls, networking events, conversations with decision makers, and sales meetings.

book a meeting for 30 minutes, I expect to be there for 30 minutes if not longer.

Aidan: That's fair. Let's pretend we didn't have to meet for the entire time if we both agreed that we'd just be filling time. How would you feel?

Stephanie: That would be great! I've got a pretty good handle on my clients and prospects, so I don't see us needing to take the entire time each week.

Aidan: Excellent. How about this: each week we will meet at 2 p.m. We're scheduled for 15 minutes. If you hit your cookbook targets, I will ask you these two questions: first, what did you learn this week that will help you be better next week, and second, what can I do to help you reach your goals? I'll expect an answer to at least the first question each week. Fair?

Stephanie: That's fair.

Aidan: If you don't hit your cookbook targets we'll spend a few minutes understanding why and how you can make up the numbers the following week. Fair?

Stephanie: Totally fair. I don't expect to have that conversation a lot.

Aidan: Great. I look forward to our meeting on Friday.

Stephanie: Me too.

Aidan: Will there be any "client issues" coming up?

Stephanie: Definitely not. If a fire does come up, it can wait until after our meeting.

Aidan: Great. See you at 2:00 p.m. on Friday.

To paraphrase our company's founder David Sandler, the problem your employee brings you is never the real problem. By seeking to understand Stephanie's real issue, Aidan went from the problem of being (supposedly) "micromanaged" to the problem of spending (supposedly) "too much time in meetings." Then he identified and dealt with the *real* issue by making a clear agreement with Stephanie about the agenda for future meetings, including an agreement that they didn't have to use the entire 15 minutes if it wasn't needed. At Sandler we call this agreement an "Up-Front Contract." This is a vitally important tool that we will discuss in more detail later in this book.

FOUR KEY QUESTIONS

Consider the following questions as you make your plans for a truly accountable team that avoids the "Big Brother" myth.

Question One: Is Your Accountability Program Excuse-Proof?

Put an intelligent animal in a new enclosure, and one of the first things that happens is the animal tests for weaknesses that would allow escape. Put an accountability program in place for your salespeople, and basically the same thing occurs. They test the system by trying to find an exception. They try to create a precedent that suggests this "flavor of the month" will pass.

The testing usually takes the form of "special" situations employees toss your way. Here's a quick, but not exhaustive, list of special situations I've encountered (and you have too).

- Child is sick
- Spouse is sick
- Parent is sick
- Pet is sick
- Salesperson is sick

- Client "emergency"
- Need time to "maintain current accounts"
- Don't know how to use the CRM effectively
- Need administrative help
- Not sure how to stick to the program
- Afraid to "do the wrong thing" (analysis paralysis)
- Don't have enough leads to meet prospecting targets
- Need a bigger territory
- Need to drop prices to compete

Lest you decide that a meaningful accountability program would be just too draconian to implement, consider the most obvious trait these "special situations" share. Most of them are *excuses* in disguise. The few that do have some shred of legitimacy (illness, say) will eventually present themselves as excuses *after* you ask your employee why he or she didn't reach the targets for the week or month.

You will notice, once you implement a real accountability program, that your "A" players, the ones you want to keep on your team, will be right up front when an issue arises in their personal or professional lives. They'll tell you ahead of time.

Your "B" and "C" players, on the other hand, will deal out these special situations like a Las Vegas casino worker whenever you shine the light on their lack of performance.

Question Two: Do You Set Accountability Targets Monthly — and Manage Them Weekly?

We recommend accountability targets to be set monthly and managed weekly. One good reason for this is that unexpected situations do arise when we need to be away to take care of a personal matter like an illness. If the absence is short-term, then that individual still has time to make up the target. If an absence is long-term, then your human resources policy takes precedence over your accountability program.

Actual client emergencies can be managed with a couple of quick questions to the client. Examples: "When were you hoping we could fix this?" and "If we can't fix the problem until later today or tomorrow, would that be OK?" After a few such questions designed to take your client from an emotional "HELP ME NOW" state to an intellectual "Actually, this isn't so bad and we can wait" state, your employee can schedule helping the client out into his day and refocus on meeting his accountability targets.

In the case of a true client emergency, the salesperson can typically either figure out a solution quickly or hand off finding a solution to a representative of the appropriate department (for instance, customer service), who keeps the salesperson updated on communications with the client.

Special situations are best dealt with up front, at the time your accountability program is implemented. Use the list of common sales "emergencies" you read above as a starting point for an in-depth discussion with your team. Set up procedures for specific situations. Close all the loopholes ahead of time! Then set accountability targets monthly — and manage them weekly.

Question Three: Do You Give Your Team Members the Tools They Need?

Providing your employees with the tools they need to succeed could mean giving written highlights of your program to certain employees who need a little more time to process changes. That way they are comfortable when the full program rolls out. You could also recruit specific "champion" employees to talk up the program and share appropriate resources prior to roll-out.

In addition, providing your team with the proper tools

means providing the right administrative support, not neces-sarily by adding new members to your team, but certainly by giving your people the proper training on how to track their own accountability targets. Quick-reference charts or FAQ documents that help create self-sufficiency in your team are also helpful.

Question Four: Do You Stick with the Program When It Hurts?

Set strong, clear up-front contracts with your employees ... then stick to your accountability program even, and especially, when it hurts. One of our clients had a problem with late arrivals to weekly meetings. The manager started locking the door to the conference room at the minute the meeting was booked to start. Within three meetings, late arrivals dropped to zero!

Exercise – Planting Your Feet

Write down one habit your team engages in that you would like to change. (Example: being late for meetings.)

_____

_____

Now write down the specific action you will take to address this problem.

_____

_____

Now write down a date, within two weeks from today, when you will tell your team face-to-face (or, if your team is remote, by phone) about the action you will take.

_____

_____

Before you implement any corrective action, it is critical that you communicate with your team, preferably face-to-face, and that the communication is based on mutually beneficial agreements, not on any need for approval from the team. This communication will be your first "plant your feet" challenge because you *will* get push-back from members of your team who are used to walking all over you!

PILLAR TWO – IMPACT ON PRODUCTIVITY

This pillar relates to how employees feel about their role in maintaining a program.

Case in Point – Top Performer Resists Accountability Program

Will is the "top" performer on Daphne's team. Daphne implemented an accountability program five weeks ago, yet Will hasn't tracked any of his agreed-upon accountability targets. Here's what a conversation with him might sound like.

Daphne: Will, I am wondering what's happening with your accountability tracking. I haven't seen any reports from you.

Will: I just can't find the time to fill the reports out each week. Besides, I'm nailing all of my deadlines, and I completed the extra Web design project you laid on me last week before it was due. When you see me start to slip, then I'll start filling out the reports.

"Top" performers like Will are running up a staircase that is falling apart behind them. They might be a star performer today, but when they experience a dip in productivity (as they inevitably do), they have no systems to fall back on that will guide them out of their dip. When his productivity does slip, Will will begin to play a game called "Look How Hard I'm Trying" with Daphne. This game is played by individuals who realize their manager is about to bring the hammer down, but who sense their manager is weak and will grant them more time to catch up on their accountabilities (when it's more likely they are looking for another job).

True top performers buy into accountability programs when they grasp the link between accountability and their own continued success. What you will quickly learn about your "top" performers when you implement an accountability program is they might actually be a "B" player in disguise — someone who will quickly jump to a new company, one that doesn't have such a defined accountability program, whenever there is pressure to perform.

YOUR BOTTOM PERFORMERS AND PRODUCTIVITY

In the world of sales, bottom performers are the "professional visitors" who make the same milk run to the same accounts week after week, with little or no increase in their book of business.

Bottom performers are the first to cite their clients as a reason why they can't follow your accountability program. You might be blessed with an employee on the bottom who, after looking at your accountability program and after considering the options elsewhere, becomes a convert, stretches his comfort zone, and turns into a solid contributor to your organization. Then again, you might not. In our experience, your bottom performers are likely to either leave your organization quickly following the implementation of a meaningful accountability program, or hang around for as long as possible before you let them go. Whether or not you opt to let them go becomes a test of the validity of your accountability program.

What your true top performers appreciate, and the rest of your employees don't, is that an accountability program actually *improves* productivity because it helps an individual employee to focus on a specific set of behaviors that will guarantee success if performed consistently.

The Bottom Line

Getting over the "Big Brother" myth of accountability requires two actions on your part:

- Learning to plant your feet and lower your need for approval with your team.
- Not accepting excuses from your team about how your accountability program will negatively impact their productivity.

THE "TOO MUCH TIME" MYTH

This myth comes primarily from leaders themselves. We have found that leaders who believe "it takes too much time" to manage an accountability program tend to enjoy being both Fire Chief and Primary Arsonist when it comes to managing their team.

Let's step outside the business world for a second. The "Too Much Time" myth believer is the equivalent of the parent who constantly hovers over a child, leaping in to help at the slightest hint of the child facing anything but a smooth, easy-to-navigate path in life. (Some call such people "helicopter parents" because of the constant hovering.) This parent keeps children close by means of various manipulative games should they ever begin down a path of independence.

What the "Too Much Time" myth believers fail to grasp is that the *only* value they have as a leader is their *time.*

ARE YOU A FIRE CHIEF?

When managers buy into the "Too Much Time" myth, they resign themselves to spending their day doing tactical coaching. This kind of coaching deals only with the problem at hand, rather than coaching strategically to ensure that the larger issue that led to the problem rarely — and preferably never — comes up again with this employee.

Case in Point – Tactical vs. Strategic Coaching

Jessie's direct report, Ryan, asks for coaching on how to resolve a conflict with an employee in another department. Watch how the discussion unfolds, first in the tactical coaching mode, and then in the strategic coaching mode.

Tactical Coaching:

Jessie: So, Ryan what can I help you with today?

Ryan: Well, I'm having problems with Bryce in Operations. I've asked for his help on a couple of projects, and he keeps throwing up roadblocks.

Jessie: What do you mean?

Ryan: Last week I asked him to look over the technical specs for a proposal I planned to send this week. He said he would, but he hasn't given me any feedback. I even sent him two emails to follow up.

Jessie: Was that the only time this happened?

Ryan: Nope. A few weeks back I popped by his office to ask a quick question for another proposal, and he blew me off.

Jessie: Blew you off?

Ryan: Yeah. He said he would get back to me, and I never heard from him.

Jessie: So what were you hoping I could do?

Ryan: I don't want you to talk to Bryce's boss. I can handle this on my own, but I don't know what to say.

Jessie: What if you said, "Bryce, the last couple times I asked for help, I didn't get what I expected. Help me understand how I should ask you for help so neither of us is disappointed."

Ryan: I think I could say that. Thanks, Jessie.

Strategic Coaching:

Jessie: So, Ryan what can I help you with today?

Ryan: Well, I'm having problems with Bryce in Operations. I've asked for his help on a couple of projects, and he keeps throwing up roadblocks.

Jessie: What do you mean?

Ryan: Last week I asked him to look over the technical specs for a proposal I planned to send this week. He said he would, but he hasn't given me any feedback. I even sent him two emails to follow up.

Jessie: Was that the only time this happened?

Ryan: Nope. A few weeks back I popped by his office to ask a quick question for another proposal, and he blew me off.

Jessie: Blew you off?

Ryan: Yeah. He said he would get back to me, and I never heard from him.

Jessie: So what were you hoping I could do?

Ryan: I don't want you to talk to Bryce's boss. I can handle this on my own, but I don't know what to say.

Jessie: That sounds like something we could figure out together, but before we go there, I'm curious why you're asking Bryce for help.

Ryan: He's the best technical person we have.

Jessie: That's true. Before you went to Bryce where did you look for the information you needed?

Ryan: Actually, I didn't. I figured that it would be quicker to ask Bryce.

Jessie: And?

Ryan: And that didn't work out the way I hoped.

Jessie: So what will you do differently next time?

Ryan: I'll start with our technical documentation.

Jessie: And if that doesn't work?

Ryan: I could ask Navid or Sean. They don't have Bryce's experience, but they're usually less busy than Bryce.

Jessie: Sounds good to me. If you did ask them for help, how would you say it? Pretend I'm them.

Ryan: I'd say something like, "Navid, I need some help. It will probably be less than five minutes. Do you have time now, or should we set something up for later?"

Jessie: Sounds good to me. What about Bryce?

Ryan: Not sure. Do I need to do anything?

Jessie: Probably not, unless you want to keep up the relationship between you two.

Ryan: I do. I like Bryce. What should I say?

Jessie: Good question. What would you say if I was Bryce?

Ryan: I'd probably say, "Hey Bryce, I think I might have asked you for help too much recently. If I did, would you be OK telling me?"

Jessie: That's worth a shot. When will you go talk to him?

Ryan: Before I leave tonight, and if he's not in his office, before lunch tomorrow.

Jessie: Great. Let me know how it goes.

From the second example, we see that the issue really isn't Bryce. It's Ryan assuming he can impose on Bryce at any time.

By coaching tactically, Jessie doesn't uncover or address the real issue. That means she will probably have this conversation with Ryan again in the near future — or at some point she will have to handle a difficult conversation with Bryce's manager, who may be well frustrated with Ryan monopolizing Bryce's time.

Coaching strategically is the exact opposite of Fire Chief coaching. Like implementing an accountability program, it takes more time in the moment, but it saves far more time in the future.

By the way, one of the benefits of implementing an effective accountability program is that, you create a common language amongst your employees, which improves their independent problem-solving ability and reduces the number and size of fires you need to fight. This is the ultimate refutation of the "Too Much Time" myth.

Most of the time spent on an accountability program is up front to design and implement, but that time is vastly outweighed by the time you will save by not fighting so many small fires each day.

ARE YOU A PRIMARY ARSONIST?

When managers who want to avoid an accountability program don't have any fires to fight, they start *looking* for fires to start with their team, so that they can swoop in to the rescue. They have no time for that accountability stuff, they'll say, because they have too many (self-started) fires to fight.

Most of the leaders I work with are dubious at first that they could ever play the role of the Primary Arsonist. Yet it's easier to fall into this pattern without realizing it than you might imagine. The most common way a manager starts a fire is by creating a special situation for the sales staff to handle. Usually this special selling situation involves a friend or relative of the manager.

Typically, the manager implies or states outright that this special situation demands immediate attention, so the team asks for help with these projects, which fulfills their manager's need to be needed while the team puts out the fire they created.

Arsonist managers have trouble creating self-sufficient teams. Even if they understand conceptually that their own time is their only valuable resource, they keep key pieces of information to themselves, which causes their employees to fail and need rescuing.

Case in Point – Keeping the Team Dependent on Their Manager

Steven's direct report, Kendra, is struggling to complete direct mail campaigns on deadline, so she goes to Steven for help.

Kendra: I'm really frustrated with our printer. I have to upload each file separately instead of batching them into one upload.

Steven: Oh, I can take care of that for you. Can you send me the files?

Kendra: Sure... they should be in your Inbox.

Steven: Perfect. And... they're uploaded.

Kendra: How did you do that?

Steven: Our printer set up my portal for batch uploading. I'm surprised they didn't do that for you.

Kendra: It's the first I heard about a batch upload option. Who do I speak with to get that set up?

Steven: Oh, I'll take care of it for you.

(Three weeks later:)

Kendra: Steve, I need to upload files for another campaign, but my portal doesn't have the batch upload function. When will that happen?

Steven: Don't worry. I'll handle the upload. Send me the files.

(Repeat until Kendra quits.)

Steven gets his needs met by Kendra needing his portal to efficiently upload files. Kendra's ability to meet her accountabilities each week is hindered by needing Steve's portal.

A more productive dialogue would include Steve agreeing to have Kendra's portal set up for batch uploading. Yet because he gets his needs met by Kendra being dependent on his portal, that conversation is unlikely to happen — or if it does happen, it's likely to end in frustration for Kendra.

The ultimate goal of any leader should be to make the team self-sufficient. A self-sufficient team essentially runs itself with minimal input from its manager. If this is a terrifying idea for you, ask yourself how much more productive and efficient you would be if you could retire your Fire Chief hat and put away your Arsonist toolkit.

Exercise – Self-Sufficiency

Write down the top three ways you could make your team more self-sufficient and a date by which you will start training them.

1. _____

_____

2. _____

_____

3. _____

_____

I commit to start making my team more self-sufficient by (date):

_____

The Bottom Line

Accountability programs only take too much time to manage if you're running around fighting or setting fires for your team. Commit to making your team self-sufficient, and you'll find plenty of time for an accountability program.

THE "VETERAN TEAM" MYTH

When we talk to managers about accountability, one of the more common push-backs is "We have a veteran team who knows what to do. We don't need to hold them accountable."

Managers who buy into the "Veteran Team" myth are afraid of two things: turnover, which we'll address next when we explore the "They'll Leave" myth, and/or getting irrefutable evidence that their veteran team doesn't know what to do.

Case in Point – Veterans Who Don't Know What to Do

The CEO of an oilfield service company implemented an accountability program for his entire sales team. His new salespeople got the program right away and consistently hit their accountability targets each week. The veteran salesperson, who had been with the company twice as long as any other salesperson and claimed to have an abundance of solid relationships with potential clients, consistently showed zeroes on his targets in the first three weeks of the program. When questioned about his results, the salesperson said he was "working on it," then quietly left the company three weeks later, thereby saving the company tens of thousands in base salary alone in the next year.

We have a saying: "They can't argue with their own data." Having a veteran team typically means relationships were built between the manager and his direct reports that go beyond business. This can make evidence of failure that much harder for a manager to accept.

To check your gut instinct that your veteran team members know what to do when it comes to their monthly activities, write down the top three activities you expect your team to do every month. These activities should simply meet your minimal expectations of job performance. Then, without sharing your list, ask each team member to write down what *he* believes are the top three activities he needs to do to just meet job performance expectations. In our experience, your list and theirs are likely to have just one match out of three, if that.

Exercise – Top Three Things

Write down the top three things you expect your team to do each month to meet your job performance expectations.

1. _____

_____

2. _____

_____

_____

3. _____

_____

It's not uncommon for veteran team members to have their own personal systems for getting the job done. These systems may have been developed out of necessity in years past, or carried over from previous employers. Many of them are deeply inefficient and irrelevant to your current situation.

Because these systems are generally incompatible with principles of accountability, transparency, or open discussion, veteran team members tend to be the ones who growl loudest when an accountability program is suggested. Managers, afraid of losing an employee's experience and knowledge, either back down from making their veteran team members follow the accountability program, or scrap the program altogether.

If your company has a track record of launching and then abandoning accountability initiatives, your veterans will take a "this too shall pass" stance until you prove to them that accountability in your company will indeed be a permanent part of the company culture going forward.

Exercise – "Flavor of the Month" Programs

In the last three years how many new programs (compensation, CRM, promotion, benefits, etc.) have you implemented with your team? _____

Of those programs, how many still exist in essentially the same form as when you implemented them? _____

The Bottom Line

The fact that your team members have a lot of experience doesn't mean that they are consistently completing the behaviors you expect them to perform in their role, or that they are all using the same system to accomplish those behaviors. Inconsistency results in inefficiency.

THE TURNOVER MYTH: "THEY'LL LEAVE"

Most leaders are terrified of turnover because they don't have any "bench strength" built up to fill the human resource holes in their organization.

When they think about implementing an accountability program, instead of visualizing themselves leaning back in their chair with their feet up on a clean desk while their self-sufficient organization attends to their accountability activities, they see their entire organization angrily marching out the door. They see themselves abandoned, solely responsible for keeping the company running.

The truth is, you will have turnover when you implement real accountability in your organization. What you'll find, though, is that the employees who leave because of the accountability program were going to leave anyway. Instead of having the guts to quit back when they mentally checked out, they've been sucking a pay check out of you every two weeks. You want these people to leave, and the sooner the better.

On the plus side, however, you are likely to notice an increase in overall team morale and productivity after the anti-accountability crowd clears out. You'll generally find that the same employees who were depleting your payroll without giving much of anything back were also depleting their colleagues' time, good will, and initiative.

Case in Point – Turnover Produces Profit Gains

The partners in an engineering firm started an accountability program after they noticed the firm's growth had slowed significantly in the last 18 months. Immediately, five out of ten employees gave notice, which put a massive amount of pressure on the firm's resources and the partners' time. Within six months of their accountability program going live, however, the firm added two new employees, growth returned to its previous pace, and profits were significantly higher with three fewer employees.

A common situation related to "They'll Leave" is the organization with a "family" atmosphere. Leaders who consider their business to be a family operation, regardless of whether or not family members are actually in the business, typically see accountability as destroying the culture they built and tearing apart the work family they helped to create. Contrary to what you may have heard, families do have accountability programs. Typically they're called "chores" or the "honey-do list," and these things don't break apart families or drive wedges between parents and children. Families are stronger *because* of accountability programs, and the organization will be as well — if the accountability programs are implemented properly.

Case in Point – "Family" Businesses

Danielle is the CEO of a 24-employee packaging manufacturer. She meets with her CFO, Richard, to discuss implementing an accountability program. Danielle is the majority shareholder, but considers Richard a mentor and greatly values his input. (Note that the key points of this discussion are relevant to sales leaders, and indeed to leaders of any team.)

Danielle: I'm concerned about productivity lately. Our defect rate is up four percent, and the shop floor is a mess.

It feels like we're getting sloppy. I plan to put some accountability measures in place to drop our defect rate and refocus the team. What do you think?

Richard: Accountability, Danielle? We're a family around here. What do we need with accountability? We hit a bump in the road recently, but I'm sure it will get sorted out. Give the team a pep talk. That's worked before.

Danielle: Pep talks worked when there were six of us, Richard. What I'm concerned about is our future. If we don't put something formal in place, we're going to be in trouble. Just because we put an accountability program in place doesn't mean we'll lose our family culture.

Richard: It just feels wrong to go all "Big Brother" on them. I'll bet most of our staff will walk if we do this.

Danielle: Richard, how many kids do you have?

Richard: Five, all grown with their own families.

Danielle: When they were little, did you let them do whatever they wanted?

Richard: No, we had some guidelines to keep them safe. Susan and I never wanted to be overly strict parents because that's what our childhoods were like.

Danielle: Did you ever let your kids choose some of the guidelines?

Richard: Sure, when they were old enough.

Danielle: And why did you do that?

Richard: We thought they would be more likely to follow the guidelines if they were their idea.

Danielle: Did you always just accept what they came up with, no questions?

Richard: Definitely not. We made the guidelines harder or softer as we saw fit.

Danielle: If your kids had the choice to leave when you put these guidelines in place, do you believe one or more of them would have?

Richard: Denise might've left. She was the rebel of the five, but she came around eventually after she thought it was her idea.

Danielle: So what if we applied the same process to implementing accountability with our team?

Richard: I guess it's worth a shot. We've always valued input from everyone, and if one or two people leave it would give us a chance to bring new people in who buy into our culture.

Danielle: Great. I'll get an all-hands meeting scheduled two weeks from now and a managers-only meeting a couple of days ahead of time.

The Bottom Line

Employees who leave because you choose to implement an accountability program with their input would have, or should have, left anyway.

In a true family organization where members of a family report to each other, accountability actually starts with an up-front contract about separating work roles and their personal roles. This is similar to a coach/athlete relationship. Outside the training ground, they are partners; inside they are coach and athlete, with both having permission to perform in those roles *without* that affecting their relationship outside of training or competition.

Turnover will happen in your organization. We suggest that, as part of your accountabilities as a manager, you should "ABR" — Always Be Recruiting. Start building your bench strength before you launch your accountability program, and you'll quickly fill the holes in your roster that are sure to pop up.

You will have turnover when you implement accountability; however, you can reduce the pain of turnover by consistently building your bench strength. Even if you don't have a strong bench after going through the short-term pain of turnover, you'll probably notice improvements in productivity and profits.

THIS CHAPTER IN 45 SECONDS

- Belief in the "Big Brother" myth occurs because of a manager's high need for approval from his team or because he believes his direct reports' claims that reporting on their accountabilities will impact their productivity.
- A manager who has a high need for approval will be overly permissive or spend too much time getting the team's opinions on decisions that the manager should make independently (e.g., standing agenda items for the team's weekly meeting).
- The first thing employees will do when an accountability program is implemented is test for weaknesses. Their testing method will create special situations for you to handle.
- Your "A" players will be up front when a special situation keeps them from hitting a target, and will take responsibility for making up their commitments.
- Your "B" and "C" players will use special situations as excuses after you expose their lack of productivity.
- True top performers embrace accountability as a way to improve themselves and demonstrate their talents.

- False "top" performers will push back on accountability because they are "making their numbers," but will switch to playing "Look How Hard I'm Trying" when their productivity dips.
- Leaders who believe that implementing accountability takes too much time are the Fire Chief and/or Primary Arsonist for their team.
- Fire Chiefs spend their time coaching tactically instead of strategically, so they waste time fighting the same fire over and over.
- Primary Arsonists *create* fires for their teams, who then must call in their Fire Chief to put out the fire.
- One of a manager's ultimate goals should be to make the team self-sufficient. Arsonists prevent their teams from self-sufficiency because they are needy.
- Veterans typically have their own way of performing in their role, which might not match your preferred system. Accountability creates a common language to get everyone on the same page and improve independent problem-solving skills, which makes your company more productive.
- If you have been guilty of implementing many programs that become the "flavor of the month" your veteran team will take a "this too shall pass" stance towards your accountability program.
- Leaders who believe the "They'll Leave" myth are guilty of not having bench strength to replace members of their team.
- To lower your anxiety when it comes to turnover, Always Be Recruiting.
- Families have accountability programs, so "family" businesses can too.

CHAPTER TWO

Start with the Mountaintop

T his is a chapter on goal setting, and if your gut reaction to that is "Not again," that's completely understandable. At this point in your career, you've probably been through too many goal-setting exercises. But like it or not, effective goal setting is vital to the success of any accountability program. So, take a deep breath, put your past goal-setting experiences behind you, and read through this chapter in its entirety *before* you begin going through the exercises. That way, you can see how each exercise fits in with the others, and by the end of the process, you'll see that goal setting can be much less painful – and much more beneficial – than you thought it could be.

David Sandler used to say, "The lead dog sets the pace." Translation: If you choose to lead, you must set the best example. If you want to implement a truly effective accountability program, your employees will need goals, not quotas — and they'll need to be comfortable sharing those goals with you. Adults learn by imitation, so by completing the exercises in this chapter you will (and must) become the model for your employees to imitate.

BEFORE YOU GO ANY FURTHER ...

Consider that a "goal" can be a fuzzy concept for some of us. Even the word "goal" can make people feel a little uneasy. So, if you find that's an issue for you as you make your way through this chapter, then instead of the word "goal," we'd invite you to think of a "mountaintop" you'd like to reach ... in a range of mountains that never ends.

A colleague of mine once gave a talk on peaks and valleys in business. One of the concepts he shared was that we tend to go into a valley because we believe we've already reached the top. High achievers understand that there really is no top of the mountain. There's just the beginning of a new climb to a new mountaintop.

So here's the reality. For accountability to exist there must be clear objectives, both ours and theirs, written down and to which you are committed. If there are no mountaintops for any of us to reach, there is ultimately *nothing* for which to be accountable. As Michelangelo put it: "The greatest danger for most of us is not that our aim is too high and we miss it, but that it is too low and we reach it."

TYPES OF GOALS

The Sander Success Triangle (on the following page) comprises three component triangles: Attitude, Behavior, and Technique. The Behavior Triangle starts with goals — specifically, with long-term, short-term, and daily/weekly goals.

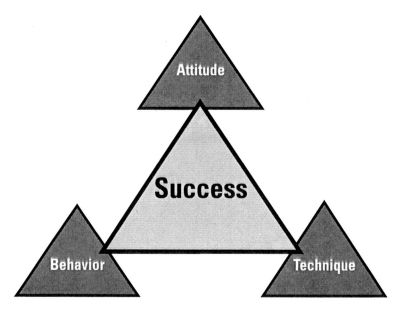

Long-Term Goals

For our purposes, long-term goals are those that you will accomplish just over two years from now. When setting long-term goals, take the day on which you are reading this book, add two years plus one day and you will have the day on which you will accomplish that goal.

There are plenty of articles that talk about 5-, 10-, and 20-year goals. But with the rate of change in our personal and professional lives looking more like a stock market chart than that of a slow, steady heartbeat, setting firm goals out beyond 3 years is an exercise in task avoidance. While there is no reason not to write down a vision statement like, "In 10 years I will have moved my business into a facility double our current size," there are so many factors outside of your control that could derail that plan that your time is best spent setting long-term goals that point you toward your vision without handcuffing you to it.

Short-Term Goals

Short-term goals are those that you will accomplish between today and two years from now. Accomplishing your short-term goals should advance you toward accomplishing your long-term goals, with flexibility to adjust along the way should outside forces dictate. (A change in government regulation would be an example of this kind of change.)

Daily/Monthly Goals

Daily/monthly goals are expressed in your behavior plan, or "cookbook," which we will discuss in the next chapter. Accomplishing these goals should advance you toward achieving your short-term goals, and should be leading, instead of lagging, indicators that you are on the path to accomplishing those goals.

Reminder: read this chapter all the way through before you attempt to complete any of the exercises.

Exercise – Goals Sub-Triangle

Score yourself 1-10 on each corner of the Goals Sub-Triangle. ("1" is low and "10" is high.) If you have at least one short- and/or one long-term goal *written down* give yourself a 10 on one or both corners. If you wrote down a "to-do" list three of the last four weeks give yourself a 10 on the daily/monthly corner.

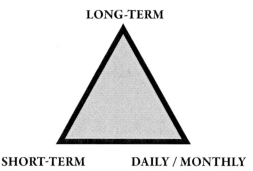

LONG-TERM

SHORT-TERM   DAILY / MONTHLY

Now that you scored yourself answer these questions:

1. In your opinion, how would your employees score themselves if you shared this exercise with them?

    _____

    _____

    _____

2. Which of your scores do you want to improve the most, and how will raising that score benefit you personally and professionally?

    _____

    _____

    _____

ARE YOU GOAL SETTING OR DAYDREAMING?

Goal achievement is *not* a linear progression from today to next week to next quarter to next year to goal achieved.

David Sandler had a rule: "You can't manage anything you can't control." The truth is, there is no shortage of things we can't control, from the economy to government regulations to technology, and lots of things in between. But if we have a clear set of goals written down, a clear plan to achieve those goals, and the discipline to stick to our plan, we will achieve our goals.

One more note important note on goals: Goals *must* be written down. If a goal isn't written down, it isn't a goal. It's a dream.

Dreams are nice, but dreams can be changed on a whim or in a moment of weak willpower. Most people don't write down their goals, and whether they realize it or not, one of the reasons they don't write goals down is that they don't want to be held accountable, even to themselves. If we write down a goal, we still feel some sense of accountability, even if we shred the piece of paper!

SEVEN AREAS OF GOALS

Just as the cliché "an overdeveloped strength becomes a weakness" has a base of truth behind it, it's also true that an obsessive focus on just one goal or aspect of your personal or professional life can cause the other areas of your life to atrophy.

I teach my clients to set goals in seven areas of their lives. Those areas are, in no particular order:

- Mind
- Body
- Spirit
- Company or Career (if you own your business this is "company")
- Social
- Family or Personal ("family" if you are in a long-term committed relationship with or without children, "personal" if not; the other goal areas cover the rest of our person)
- Financial

Mind Goals

Mind goals relate to what you put, or don't put, into your mind. This includes reading non-fiction books, watching documentaries, taking a course at a local post-secondary institution, or visiting a museum. A challenge I put to all of my clients, which I will share with you, is this: read 15 pages of a non-fiction book related to your business every business day, and take the weekends off to read fiction or catch up on TV. At the end of one year you will have read roughly 12 non-fiction books related to your business, which will put you several steps ahead of your competitors.

Exercise – Mind Goals

Note: Before you write down your first set of goals, remember; consider that each goal should contain the following two attributes:

- ***Strong goals are stated in the present tense*** – *"I want to quit smoking" becomes, "I am a non-smoker." "I want to lose 10 pounds" becomes, "I am at my ideal weight of (10 pounds less than you are)." This is to trick your brain into helping you achieve your goals, which is discussed in more detail at the end of this chapter. If you can't bring yourself to write your goals in the present tense use the future affirmative tense, "I will..."*
- ***Strong goals are written in a positive tone*** – *Instead of "I won't eat sweets," your goal is "I choose real food over processed snacks." Instead of "I won't drink so much," your goal is "I drink in moderation." Goals that are written in the negative tend to fail because they remind us of our parents smacking our hand (figuratively or literally), which triggers a rebellious response in us.*

Write down two short-term and two long-term goals for your mind. You'll need these goals and the other goals you set in the other six areas later in this chapter.

Short-term (<2 years)	Long-term (>2 years)
1.	1.
2.	2.

Body Goals

Body goals are specific to three core areas of your body – sleep, diet, and exercise. Some of my clients have asked me to help them put together "body cookbooks." A core component of each cookbook was tracking how many nights per week they slept uninterrupted from the time they closed their eyes to the time they woke up, either by alarm or on their own. Plenty of recent research has illustrated the negative implications of attempting to function on too little sleep for too long.

Along with getting enough sleep (seven to eight hours per night), your diet and exercise will also be a leading indicator of how successful you are at accomplishing your goals. Mom said "Eat your breakfast" for a reason. A proper breakfast, one that doesn't consist mostly of simple carbohydrates and caffeine, gives your body and brain the energy they need to operate at 100 percent effectiveness, at least until mid-morning.

Exercising — even skipping rope for one minute at a time in your office, which is one of my ways to recharge — helps clear your mind, allows your subconscious to work on big problems, and actually restores your energy. How often do you feel energized after exercising? Maybe not at the moment you stop, but shortly after exercising, your body's efforts to repair the micro-damage done to your muscles makes you feel recharged.

The key with body goals is to start small and build up from there. Going from nothing to "I'll take the four flights of stairs to the office every morning" is a quick way to burn out. Make your goal taking the stairs once per week for two weeks. You'll probably take the stairs more often than that on your own initiative before the two weeks are up.

Exercise – Body Goals

Write down two short-term and two long-term goals for your body.

Short-term (< 2 years)	*Long-term (>2 years)*
1.	1.
2.	2.

Spirit Goals

Spirit goes do not have to mean "religion." Spirit simply means a belief in something more than yourself. For some of my clients, going for a hike in the mountains is a spiritual experience because it connects them with something greater than themselves. Several clients feel the same way about practicing yoga. If you do belong to an organized religion, a spirit goal could relate to how often you attend your house of worship or how closely you abide by the conduct codes specified by your religion. Establishing a routine of prayer and/or meditation is another way to attain spirit goals.

Exercise – Spirit Goals

Write down two short-term and two long-term goals for your spirit.

Short-term (<2 years)	*Long-term (>2 years)*
1.	1.
2.	2.

Company and/or Career Goals

It makes no sense to set goals if you're not personally in the position to make them happen, so company goals will only apply to you if you're a business owner or majority shareholder. Even as the chief executive of a billion dollar enterprise, though you might have some say in the goals of the company, ultimately those goals are not really goals, but quotas given to you. We'll talk more about the difference between goals and quotas later in this chapter.

When considering career goals, it's important to tailor those goals to you and your particular needs. Not everyone wants to be the chief executive. Setting a career goal requires you to have a frank conversation with yourself about how much responsibility you want to take on, how work will affect your planned or current relationships or family situation, as well as an honest appraisal of how well you manage stress.

If you are the owner of your business, a company goal, especially in the long term, should relate to the growth of your business — whether that be in number of employees, revenue, profit, market share, or new products.

There is no reason to be ashamed of growth. As David Sandler said, "If you aren't growing, you're dying."

Exercise – Company or Career Goals

Write down two short-term and two long-term goals for your company or career.

Short-term (< 2 years)	Long-term (> 2 years)
1.	1.
2.	2.

Social Goals

There are two kinds of social goals.

The first is your relationship with your friends and non-work, non-family associates. Think about the relationships you had with your closest friends in high school and/or college. If you gave each of those relationships a "10" at the time, what would they be now?

Second is your relationship with your community, specifically as it relates to volunteering and philanthropy.

A side note is in order here. Personal goals relate to your personal growth and development outside of the other goal areas outlined in this chapter. A personal goal does *not* have to be "get into a relationship," although it could be. You could also set a personal goal to climb Mount Kilimanjaro, backpack through Southeast Asia, or become fluent in a new language. Personal goals usually touch on or directly cross over with mind, body, or spirit goals.

Exercise – Social Goals

Write down two short-term and two long-term social goals.

Short-term (<2 years)	Long-term (>2 years)
1.	1.
2.	2.

Family Goals

Family goals relate to your relationship with your family, as far as you would like to extend the definition of that word. You might define your family as you, your spouse, your children (if any), your parents, and your spouse's parents. Your family goals will also focus on time spent with your family and/or specific family activities like vacations.

Exercise – Family Goals

Write down two short-term and two long-term goals for you or your family.

Short-term (< 2 years)	Long-term (> 2 years)
1.	1.
2.	2.

Financial Goals

When working with clients, we find that financial goals are often the trickiest to discuss because of the negative messages about money some of us received from our parents and other authority figures when we were children. Examples of such scripting might include "It's rude to talk about money," or "Money doesn't grow on trees." It seems that many of my clients set financial goals as if they were spinning a roulette wheel and were satisfied with whatever number on which their ball lands. That's not the best approach.

Financial goals can relate to any aspect of your finances. For example, when I completed my program at Douglas College, my number one financial goal was paying off all of my student debt as fast as possible. While achieving that goal meant I hit "pause" on starting a retirement savings program, becoming debt-free two years after completing my first post-secondary program meant I ultimately had more money available to invest for my retirement instead of continuing to dump it into interest payments.

When setting your financial goals, be sure to ask and answer the question "Why?" for each one. For example, a common financial goal we hear from our clients is "I want to double my income." That sounds like a great goal, but why is doubling important to you? What happens if you achieve that goal, both positively (more options) and negatively (more taxes)? What would happen if you earned 1.5 times your income from last year to this year? The consequences of a financial goal, both positive and negative, must be thought through before you commit to that goal.

Exercise – Financial Goals

Write down two short-term and two long-term goals for your finances.

Short-term (<2 years)	*Long-term (>2 years)*
1.	1.
2.	2.

WHY YOU SHOULD TALK ABOUT YOUR GOALS

The next step is to communicate your goals to someone else. You communicate your goals to enlist the help of others in accomplishing those objectives. If your goals or expectations are never (or poorly) communicated, then others will not be able to help you get the results that you want.

Lots of people have personal goals or aspirations. What they usually don't do is share those goals with their friends and acquaintances. The special thing about people is that they will go out of their way to help a person even if there is only a hint of need. If you tell someone about one of your goals, that person typically provides ideas or suggests resources that can help you to accomplish the goal. It only makes sense that you should really share your goals with everyone you meet.

What goal have you not shared with those you know? Why haven't you shared that goal? What would happen if you did share your goal? If you haven't already, take a chance and consciously share your goals and see what happens. Repeat this sharing with others until it becomes an attitude and habit. See how your progress quickens toward the results you want.

LIFELINE

We all want more time. More time with our family. More time with our friends. More time with ourselves. Yet time passes constantly and we are the ones who choose what to make of the time we have.

When we consider our goals, we have to consider where we are in our lives in order to map out a realistic timeline for completing them. To illustrate this point, David Sandler used the Lifeline exercise.

Exercise – Your Lifeline

Draw a horizontal line about six inches long on a separate piece of paper, or use the one provided below.

Underneath the line on the left-hand side draw a capital "B" and above it, write down the year you were born.

Move right from the "B," and one to three inches down the

line, draw a capital "T" below the line and above that, write today's date, including the current year.

Move right from "T" an additional one to two inches and draw a capital "R" below the line. Above the "R" write down the year you want to retire. (By our definition "retire" doesn't mean that you have to stop working, but just that you could if you wanted to.)

Go to the far right of the line and underneath the line draw a capital "D." Above that write down the year you expect to die. Now cross out that number and add 10 years — my gift to you. This is usually the second hardest part of the exercise for most people, which is totally fair. No one wants to think about dying, but it will happen to all of us eventually.

Next draw an "X" through the line between "B" and "T." Everything up to today is in the past. All of your successes, failures, scripts, head trash, lessons learned, and regrets are contained in that space. If I could redo my time between "B" and "T," I would choose to fail faster.

Now consider the point between "T" and "R," but don't change anything. Finally, look back at all of the goals you just set for yourself. In the space below write down how you feel about the time you have between "T" and "R" in which to accomplish the goals you've set for your working life. Where you are in your life will dictate a lot of your emotion about this exercise.

Given that you only have a finite amount of time between "T" and "R," what adjustments, if any, will you make to your goals, and what specific, measurable steps will you take in the next week to start achieving them?

_____

_____

_____

_____

_____

_____

_____

Vision Boards

For some people, writing down goals still doesn't make them "real." For the visually oriented among us, we recommend creating a vision board, also known as a dream board, with pictures attached that represent your goals. My vision board hangs next to my computer to remind me of my personal mountaintops. If I have a moment of task avoidance, a look at my vision board gives me a boost to keep moving towards achieving my goals.

Exercise – Cut and Paste

If you're unsure how to get started with a vision board, first buy a large piece of poster board or a cork board.

Next buy magazines that contain visual representations of your goals (new house, new car, tropical vacation, engagement ring, etc.) or use your favorite search engine to find pictures online.

Once you gather your pictures, cut them out and glue them to your poster board or use thumb tacks to stick them to your cork board.

Hang your vision board where you will see it every day. David Sandler recommended hanging it in your bathroom so you could see it every time you brushed your teeth.

This is a fun exercise to do with your family. Many of my colleagues invite the families of their clients to a special training session in December each year where everyone creates their own vision board. Building a vision board is an effective way to not only make your goals feel more tangible, but also to remind you of those goals on an ongoing basis. If your goals seem like abstractions, or if you allow them to fade into the back of your mind, you're much less likely to do what's necessary on a day-to-day basis to make them a reality.

PRIORITIZING YOUR GOALS

High achievers don't reach their levels of success by doing everything at once. They have a tightly focused ranking of priorities that helps them sort through their weeks, months, and years while steadily moving forward towards the next mountaintop in their personal mountain range.

Most people tend to prioritize by how shiny the object is or how quickly they believe they could accomplish a goal. Winners, on the other hand, prioritize by the long-term value that accomplishing a specific goal will bring them, their family, and/or their business.

Prioritizing helps us understand what we value most in life, and our values tend to indicate where we spend our time. For example, if one of your goals is "double my business," which you rank number two, and another goal is "spend quality time with my children," which you rank number four, we can see what will take priority when you have a conflict between doubling your business and spending quality time with your children. You will focus on work over family.

SHORT-TERM VS. LONG-TERM

Because priorities change over time, we recommend ranking your short-term and long-term goals independently. For many parents, spending quality time with their children is a priority when their children are younger and have fewer activities outside their home. As his children grow, a parent's goal priorities may shift because he isn't spending as much time with his children. Where a goal fits into your priorities depends on where you are in your life. If you take the time to place your priorities appropriately, you'll find it much easier to choose the right path when multiple goals are fighting for your time.

YOUR GOALS OR MINE?

One roadblock my clients sometimes raise when we do the prioritizing exercise is potential for conflicts with their spouse's or partner's goals. While this is a valid concern on the surface, what lies below this fear is a lack of communication.

As we have seen, a critical part of setting goals is to share those goals with others. What we see time and time again in movies, on television, and in novels is often that one person in a partnership selflessly puts his goals aside to support the goals of his partner. While this may seem a noble gesture on the surface, it can often lead to feelings of profound resentment — and possibly the end of the partnership. While it's rarely possible for both parties in a relationship to accomplish all of their goals, that doesn't mean that one of you must sacrifice everything. With proper communication and planning, both of you can accomplish more. Not only that, but your relationship will be stronger because you've worked toward your goals together.

One year when I worked for Canada NewsWire, I set a goal

of doubling my income from the previous year. My wife was in the middle of her Master's degree at the time. We sat down and had a conversation about our goals, the benefits to us if I achieved my goal, and the behaviors I would need to do to accomplish that goal. All of this, we realized, meant less time together for about a year. We needed to make that decision together. We mutually agreed that it made sense for me to pursue that goal, and in the next 12 months I more than doubled my income. Had I made that call on my own, resentments might have built up, and our relationship might have suffered. Because we went into the next year understanding the sacrifices up front, however, we not only accomplished our goals, but we also had the satisfaction of having accomplished something important together.

Share this chapter with your life partner, if you have one. Suggest that he or she complete the same exercises, and discuss your responses together afterwards. While you will likely have a difficult conversation in some places, you will ultimately be further ahead on achieving your goals if you and your partner are on the same page.

Exercise – Ranking Your Goals

Select one of the two short-term and long-term goals you wrote down under each of the seven goal categories and rank them one to seven. Rank one list first and then rank the other.

Short-term (< 2 years)	Long-term (>2 years)
1. _____ _____	1. _____ _____
2. _____ _____	2. _____ _____
3. _____ _____	3. _____ _____
4. _____ _____	4. _____ _____
5. _____ _____	5. _____ _____
6. _____ _____	6. _____ _____
7. _____ _____	7. _____ _____

DISCIPLINED BEHAVIOR, CONSISTENT RESULTS

While ranking a goal as number six on your list *doesn't* mean you won't accomplish it, it *does* mean that accomplishing that goal might take longer than you expected, which could impact your motivation for accomplishing that goal.

To illustrate think of a friend who had an ambitious, short-term, personal goal. Maybe that friend planned to lose eight pounds in one month or wanted to save enough money to go on an all-inclusive vacation in the next quarter.

That friend probably started out really motivated, by creating an exercise and diet plan to the letter or setting up an auto-deduct transaction through his bank that instantly put a specific amount of money away in a savings account.

About halfway through your friend's specified time period, it's possible he started to feel some personal doubt. There was a disconnect between the progress that *had been* made toward the goal and the progress your friend thought *should have been made* by that point.

If our behavior is disciplined and consistent, our results will be consistent. If our behavior is erratic, our results will be erratic.

Perhaps your friend stuck to the plan and achieved the goal slightly later than his original deadline. What often happens, though, is people start to doubt themselves, doubt their plan, and begin to panic, and then they attempt quick fixes to jump ahead — which actually puts them behind. Then they double down on their original plan to catch up, and eventually they give up because they feel nothing is working and it's pointless to continue.

Prioritizing your goals helps to prevent this cycle. It helps you understand what is important to you at that moment in time ... and focus on achieving the goals that are most important to you.

GOALS VS. QUOTAS

As I mentioned earlier, a goal is a mountaintop that you define for yourself. A quota, on the other hand, is a goal that is given to you. As a rule, a goal is more motivating than a quota.

A harsh truth about your employees is that they don't work for your organization because they love your company. They work for your company because they believe that working for you helps them achieve their goals faster than working for someone else.

Don't get nervous. Your employees aren't going to leave en masse tomorrow. What you might want to ponder, though, is this question: how can you tap into your employees' internal motivation to achieve their quotas?

Quotas are a part of business. It is a rare company that creates a long-term, sustainable business on the instructions "Go sell stuff" and "Go make stuff."

Employees complain about quotas. This isn't new. You might have done it yourself before you were promoted to management or before you started your own business. What's challenging is drawing a correlation between an employee's quota, the benefit to the company, and the benefit to the employee.

If your compensation plan boils down to "Hit this quota or you're fired," then this book won't help you!

Case in Point – Tying Quotas Back to Goals

Darren is the owner of an electrical supply business who shared targets with his sales team last week. Josh, the second highest performer on the sales team last fiscal year, isn't happy about his targets:

Darren: Thanks for coming in at our scheduled time, Josh. What's up?

Josh: I'm really struggling with the targets you gave me last week.

Darren: Help me understand. What do you mean?

Josh: I get that you want to be aggressive in moving into larger orders, but you're asking me to basically double my sales next year.

Darren: OK. That makes sense. Where's the struggle happening?

Josh: I'm now sure from where these extra sales are going to come. We're the most expensive supplier out there and most of us have maxed out our territories.

Darren: Maxed out?

Josh: Yeah, we're selling about as much as we can to our existing customers, and new customers seem to all be rabbits buying little bits here and there, but nothing consistent.

Darren: Hmm. Josh, tell me: where did you rank on the team in sales last year?

Josh: I was number two, barely behind Sheila.

Darren: How do you feel about that?

Josh: I'm OK being number two to Sheila. She's awesome, but I don't like being number two generally.

Darren: Because?

Josh: Because I like winning. When I played lacrosse, I won at every level.

Darren: But you're going to not win against the target set for next year?

Josh: Oh. Um.

Darren: That's OK. I got to a comfortable spot in my career about 12 years ago and hung out there for a while. It took being passed by too many chargers like you to shake me out of it and go start this company.

Josh: OK, let's say that I take a shot at this target and fail. What then?

Darren: Fair question. What would you do if our positions were switched and that happened?

Josh: It depends on how close you got. If you totally blew it and only got to 70 or 75 percent, I'd probably fire you. If you did at least 80 percent, that would take you above where you got last year and I'd keep you.

Darren: Sounds fair to me. How can I help you get started?

Josh: I've got a couple of ideas to pull the trigger on next week, but I'd like some time with you to map out how I get from 80 to 100 percent of this target.

Darren: I look forward to hearing how those ideas turn out, bad or good. Do you have your calendar handy? Let's book that time right now.

KNOW THEIR GOALS

To make quotas work, you must understand your employees' goals — their true motivation for working for you.

We already identified that not everyone wants to be the chief executive, earn a million dollars in one year, send their children to private school, and live in a new mansion every few years.

Our goals are *our* goals, whether they be large or small in the eyes of others. Your employees may be reluctant to share their goals out loud because they fear judgment. Guess what? Knowing *their* goals means first helping them to understand *your* goals.

This might be a terrifying thought for you. Sharing your goals with your employees sounds like weakness. In reality, being vulnerable enough to share your goals with your employees is what displays your strength as a leader. Being vulnerable with your employees also makes them more likely to trust you because you put yourself on a human-to-human level with them.

You don't have to share your deepest desires, hopes, and dreams with your employees. Keep your communication professional, but open up enough for your team to see that you face similar challenges to theirs when you are considering the next mountaintop to tackle.

Exercise – Sharing Your Goals

Write down one short-term and one long-term goal, personally and professionally, that you will share with your team at your next meeting.

Personal	Professional
1.	1.
2.	2.

After you've shared your goals, open the meeting for questions about those goals, and close this agenda item with a suggestion that someone else share four of his goals at the next meeting.

By sharing your goals first and inviting questions, you model for your team that goal setting and vulnerability are important parts of your organization's culture.

How Your Brain Can Help or Hurt Goal Achievement

I believe our brain can be an enemy or an ally in achieving our goals, but because of the way we talk about our goals, we often turn our brain against us.

Here's something to consider. In the average human, our brain is about two percent of our total body weight, yet it consumes 20 percent of the energy we burn daily. Because our brain is such an energy pig, it jealously guards against threats that could reduce the amount of energy available to it.

At the same time, our brain is wired like an animal. It lives in the moment and can only draw from past experiences to predict the future. As Mark Twain said, "If a cat sits on a hot stove, that cat won't sit on a hot stove again. It won't sit on a cold stove either."

This creates a "want/will" paradox when we talk about our goals. Ask a group of friends what their goals are, and they'll likely start off with "I want to..." or "I'd like to..." That's not the kind of language on which the brain thrives.

Think back to when you were a child or to what you say to your children today. Were you asked, "What *will* you be when you grow up?" or "What do you *want* to be when you grow up?" I was asked the latter. I didn't much like the question.

In my view, when your brain hears "want" as in "I want to lose 10 pounds" or "I want to double my client base," it does a quick calculation and decides, "If I 'want' it, that means I don't have it, and it sounds like I'd need to burn a lot of energy to get it. That's energy that won't be available for brain function — so let's pass on that idea."

What happens next is that you may start out with good intentions — following your exercise program for a few weeks — but your brain will eventually override your willpower, convincing you to "take a rest day." This is task avoidance, which will cause you to fall short of your goal.

On the other hand, if you tell your brain you *will* lose 10 pounds (or double your client base, or whatever), your brain does the same calculation and decides, "This is already in process, but I don't quite have it yet, so let's figure out how to burn the right amount of energy to get there."

By *willing* yourself toward a goal you recruit your brain's energy into task *achievement* instead of task *avoidance*.

I believe the most terrifying word for your brain is "need," as in "I *need* to hire a new assistant" or "I *need* to exercise." To your brain "need" triggers your "fight or flight" response as in "I need to move from the path of that oncoming car." To your brain "need" means "I have to give up the energy I want in order to ensure survival."

Because your brain has no history of hiring an assistant being necessary for your survival, it shifts you from task completion to task avoidance by creating a shiny object for you to chase that doesn't require much energy. For instance: "Let's rearrange my desk."

To trick your brain into being your ally, start writing your goals as "I will." Use "will" instead of "want" and "need" when you talk about your goals.

Exercise – Want vs. Will

Go back to double-check the goals you wrote down under the seven categories listed earlier in this chapter.

If you wrote the word "want" next to any goal, cross it out.

Next, write the words "I will" beside each goal you wrote down. Grammar doesn't matter.

This Chapter in 45 Seconds

- Think of goals as mountaintops in a range that never ends.
- We hit valleys in our businesses because we believe that we've reached a peak.
- Winners understand there are no peaks, just the base of the next mountaintop.
- Three primary types of goals are long-term (to be accomplished in just over two years), short-term (to be accomplished in two years or less), and daily/monthly.
- Daily/monthly goals are your leading indicators that tell you if you are on pace to reach your short-term goals.
- Sandler suggests you set short- and long-term goals in each of the following categories:
  - Mind
  - Body
  - Spirit
  - Company or Career
  - Social
  - Family or Personal
  - Financial
- Share your goals with everyone you meet; you'll find help in unlikely places.
- The time between "today" and when you'd like to "retire" is the time you have to hit your working life goals.
- Prioritize your goals to help you focus your energy and attention.
- Prioritizing your goals doesn't mean you won't achieve the

goals at the bottom of your rankings, but it does mean it will probably take you a longer period of time to achieve them.

- A goal is a mountaintop that you define for yourself. A quota is a goal that is given to you. A goal is more motivating than a quota.

- Your employees work for you not because they love your organization, but because working for you helps them achieve their goals.

- Our goals are *our* goals, whether they are large or small in the eyes of others.

- At your next meeting, you should share two business and two personal goals with your team.

- Your brain can either help or hinder the achievement of your goals.

- Remember the want/will paradox when writing or speaking about your goals.

CHAPTER THREE

The Path to the Mountaintop

I dentifying mountaintops is a great initial step, but that's all it is: an initial step. If you've attempted to achieve even *one* important goal in your life, though, you already know that the path to the top of that mountain isn't likely to be a straight line.

High achievers understand that the fastest way to reach any given mountaintop is to sketch out a path that defines the specific, measurable *behaviors* required to reach it — and also the amount of each behavior required, on a monthly basis, to get there.

What prevents people from actually defining and reaching their mountaintops? They get stuck in the procrastination triangle.

PROCRASTINATION TRIANGLE

Have you ever said, "I'll get to that tomorrow" when it came to taking action on your important goals for the coming year? Did you say that on January 2? January 10? Did you wait all the way to the Super Bowl before giving up?

If you've ever fallen short of a goal because of this kind of internal dialogue, or if you have noticed that you are on pace to fall short at some point before December 31 and have put off taking any meaningful action on the goal, you're trapped in the procrastination triangle.

Draw an equal sided triangle. Label the top "no goals," the bottom left "no plan," and the bottom right "no discipline." (See the diagram.)

NO GOALS

NO PLAN   **NO DISCIPLINE**

Now score yourself from 1 to 10 on each corner. In this case, a lower score is best. For example, a "1" for "no goals" means, "I now have goals written down for my business and personal life," while a "10" means, "I've heard that some people have goals."

A "1" for "no plan" means, "I have a clear plan written down to achieve each of my goals," and a "10" means, "I rely on hope and luck to reach my goals."

A "1" for "no discipline" means, "I do what's on my plan every week," while a "10" means, "Meh, I'll get to it eventually."

Be brutally honest. After you score yourself, total up your scores and check the key on the following page to find out how likely you are to procrastinate your way out of success.

Score Key:

- **3-9** – You'll occasionally fall victim to task avoidance, but generally you stick to your plan and hit your goals.
- **10-21** – You probably have a problem with discipline, which is probably compounded by a lack of clear goals and/or the lack of a specific plan to achieve them. Find an accountability partner and commit to a plan that will lower your score.
- **22-30** – Buff up your LinkedIn® profile because unless you set goals, create a plan, and bring some discipline into your life, you'll soon be looking for a new job (and possibly a new place to live).

Without clear business and personal goals, a specific plan to achieve each of your goals broken down to weekly activities, and the discipline to complete your plan week in and week out, you won't be successful. It's that simple.

We tackled the "goals" part of the triangle in the previous chapter. In this chapter we'll tackle the "plan" and "discipline" parts of the equation.

MANAGE BEHAVIOR, NOT NUMBERS

One of David Sandler's most important rules was "Never manage your numbers. Manage your behavior." This advice runs counter to traditional management practices.

While "managing by spreadsheet" still happens, the most common way we manage by numbers is by looking at outputs, also known as lagging indicators, such as "closed deals." These don't give a true picture of a business until you collect between three to six months' worth of information. Instead, we should be looking at leading indicators, such as "new contacts with whom I set up-front contracts for an initial meeting," which can provide a clear picture of the health of your business in just three to six weeks.

There's a big difference between lagging indicators and leading indicators. If your organization was a yacht that had sprung a leak, a lagging indicator would be how much water came into your yacht *yesterday*. A leading indicator, on the other hand, would be how much water is coming in *right now*. The former is interesting; the latter is potentially life-saving.

For most managers, managing behavior instead of numbers requires a major mind shift. That shift is worth making, though, because, just like a coach in professional sports, your primary function as a manager is to improve the performance of your team. Unfortunately, traditional approaches to performance management and accountability don't do this in a way that is sustainable over time.

WHY TRADITIONAL PERFORMANCE MANAGEMENT DOESN'T WORK

Traditional performance management approaches tend to look like this:

- **What did the manager before me do?** – Also known as the "hope and pray" approach. This approach is typically used by a manager who is either unprepared to be thrust into a managerial role or told to "hold the line" by the boss. The problem with this approach is that, if the team succeeds, it will be *in spite* of, not *because* of, this manager's efforts.

- **What's the opposite of what the manager before me did?** – This is the "change agent" approach, typically used by managers who are brought in to "shake things up." The problem with this approach is that it assumes the *entire* team is broken, so this manager not only loses "C" players, who can't keep up with the changes implemented, but also "A" players, who feel they are being punished for the failures of their colleagues.

- **What did my manager do to me?** – This is the "doomed to repeat history" approach. As children learn how to behave by watching their parents, these managers learn how to manage from their past managers. Now, either these manager *liked* how they were managed and mimic their former manager's style, or they *disliked* how they were managed, and so manage opposite to their former manager's style. This approach is typically used by managers with no previous managerial experience, or who are in a newly created role and thus can't use the first or second approach. Entrepreneurs often adopt this approach. The problem with either side of this approach is that it doesn't consider the team that is *currently* being managed.

Believe it or not, all of these approaches can provide varying degrees of initial success. The challenge with sustaining that success has to do with your most valuable asset as a manager — your *time*. Without a performance management and accountability system in place, you will eventually get sucked into a time vortex created by mid- and low-performing team members who require constant supervision and re-training.

The alternative to the traditional approaches is to implement a performance management system that both empowers team members to perform at their highest level — *and* gives you time back in your week so you can focus on coaching and mentoring your team. What I'm about to share with you delivers positive results even if you can only devote 20 minutes a week to each of your team members!

Your Performance Management System

An effective sales performance management system has three parts:

- **Funnel management** – Here you break your team's process (be it sales, operations, customer service, human resources, or anything else) into parts, and assign percentages between each stage that show how many "inputs" (for instance, first calls to prospects) are needed to create how many "outputs" (for instance, closed sales). A great funnel management system also contains checklists for each stage that *must* be completed before advancing to the next stage. By creating a sound funnel management process, you will get time back in your week because your team won't waste your time with "special requests" to skip a step in your process by, for instance, asking for a discount off your rate card.

- **Monthly behavior plan** – As we have seen, a behavior plan is called a "cookbook." A cookbook is created by each team member, approved by you, and contains all of the behaviors that must be completed on a monthly basis in order to perform in the role: the number of prospecting calls, meetings with prospects, networking events, etc. Note that a target must be assigned to each behavior. Cookbook targets are set monthly and tracked weekly. (We'll get to the reason for this a little later in this chapter.)

- **Personalized development plan** – Without a development plan personalized to each member of your team, you will spend a lot of time working on effects, rather than causes, and you'll waste both their time and yours. Even your superstars who nail the first two parts of your performance management system will eventually fail, or become dissatisfied and leave, if you don't provide them with a unique development path.

Here's a surprise: the best development plans are created by third parties. These can be from a consultant, or they can be based on surveys like the Devine Inventory™. Third-party plans significantly reduce or eliminate the bias inherent in self-evaluation forms or so-called "360 degree" reviews compiled by people who work with the salesperson.

Performance management and accountability systems are vital, and successfully implementing this kind of system is a good start. Yet stopping here would be like stopping after building the foundation of your house. There's more to be done.

WHAT ARE YOUR CRUCIAL NUMBERS?

The crucial numbers for you to define are the leading indicators.

To start tracking your leading indicators, you must have the process you are analyzing (sales, operations, accounting, marketing, whatever) written down and broken up into defined parts.

Part of defining your process is specifying how long, on average, each stage in the process should take. For example, in a sales process, if the time between step one (the discovery meeting) and step two (where you present the results of network analysis) is an average of two weeks, and you notice you have a bottleneck of opportunities sitting at step one for three, four, or five weeks, that is a leading indicator of a problem.

The fastest way to double your team's sales is to cut your sales cycle in half. That doesn't mean that you can literally cut your time from first contact to close by 50 percent, but it does mean that you can look for ways to prevent opportunities from dragging on and on beyond the typical cycle. This can only be done, however, if your sales process is clearly defined.

Other leading indicators Sandler clients track for their sales team include:

- **Average deal size** – Monitoring your average deal size is a good leading indicator of your sales team's current preference for hunting so-called rabbits, meaning small deals that close quickly, or whales, meaning large deals that take longer to close.

- **Meeting completion percentage** – The single biggest cost of sales can be found in appointments that get booked, but never happen — usually after a salesperson has travelled to the prospect's office and waited 10-20 minutes before being told the meeting is off. The salesperson makes the trip and travels back again. All or part of the day is shot. What can you do to improve this metric?

- **"Proposal" rate** – Here, "proposal" means "advancing the prospect down our sales funnel." This metric helps you as a manager understand whether your team is booking a lot of meetings with unqualified prospects ... or disqualifying a potential client too quickly.

- **Meeting conversion rate** – Getting conversations with decision makers is great, but if your team isn't converting those conversations to discovery meetings, your entire sales process stops.

- **Conversation rate** – Measures a salesperson's success in converting prospecting attempts into conversations with decision makers. This metric can be broken down by prospecting attempt (prospecting calls, walk-ins, networking, referral requests, etc.).

- **Number of unique conversations with decision makers** – A crucial number that helps you understand whether

your salespeople actually get to speak with decision makers
... or are getting stalled by gatekeepers, or calling lower in a
prospect organization, where they feel more comfortable.

IF YOU HAVE NO LEADING INDICATORS

One of my clients approached me about setting up an accountability plan, but didn't know where to start. His biggest problem
was that he didn't know what behaviors he should include in his
accountability plan because he wasn't tracking anything when
we started working together.

The plan we came up with included a four-week behavior
tracking study of the sales, marketing, and customer service departments. Each person in those departments, from manager to
most junior employee, would spend the next two weeks tracking
the behaviors completed each day to help the company grow and
maintain its client base: taking inbound customer support calls,
writing blog posts, attending networking events, or whatever else
fit the description.

At the end of the study we analyzed the results, culled out the
specific, measurable behaviors for each department, and implemented an accountability program that was specific to the department and individual.

Exercise – Crucial Numbers

Write down the name of a department or team in your company. Pick three leading indicators you will track over the next
90 days. If you pick your sales department, use three behaviors
relevant to growing and maintaining the client base. Review the
"If You Have No Leading Indicators" section above to generate
some ideas.

Department:

_____

_____

Leading indicator #1:

_____

_____

Leading indicator #2:

_____

_____

Leading indicator #3:

_____

_____

Next to each leading indicator above, write down what you believe that number to be right now (for instance, 50 percent or 40,000). Those numbers will give you a base to analyze your actual data 90 days from now.

Exercise – Behavior Tracking Study

If you are still unsure about what behaviors to include in your cookbook, you can use the following template to complete a four-week behavior tracking study within one department. Everyone in the department participates, from manager to most junior employee. Examples of behaviors to track include processing accounts payable, writing blog posts, shooting promotional video, debugging code, cleaning production equipment, or making outbound prospecting calls.

Name:

Department:

Role:

Behavior (Activity)	Amount in Week 1	Amount in Week 2	Amount in Week 3	Amount in Week 4

Once you complete your study, take a look at the data for key behaviors that you believe will lead to continued growth in your company. Key behaviors should appear regularly in your study. For example, "cleaning production equipment" is a key behavior that ensures your machines operate at maximum efficiency and provides an opportunity to identify potential maintenance issues before they cause breakdowns.

BUILDING A LEADER'S COOKBOOK

As a leader, you're in the people development business. Unless you still perform a business task in your organization (sales, operations, accounting, etc.), your cookbook should focus *entirely* on developing your people.

Sandler clients who successfully implement accountability programs have a manager/leader cookbook that includes some or all of the following:

- **Group Accountability Meetings (GAMs)** – Not your traditional sales meeting, which often gets referred to as a WPK (weekly posterior-kicking) session. A group accountability meeting is part cookbook pre-mortem — a discussion about what will prevent each team member from hitting his targets this week — and part group problem-solving session with you as facilitator.
- **Weekly Individual Meetings (WIMs)** – A WIM is a personal cookbook review/coaching session with each of your direct reports, twice per week. It usually takes the form of five minutes on Monday morning spent answering the question, "What will you accomplish this week?" and 15 minutes on Friday answering the questions, "What did you accomplish? What prevented you from reaching that/

those target(s)? and How can I help you make up those numbers next week?" You really can create an accountability mentality for your team members, and a leadership mentality for yourself, in just twenty minutes a week!

- **Role-play** – The fastest way to create change in your people is through role-play. Yes, this means you must participate personally in the role-play exercises. By using role-play to model the behavior you want to see from your direct reports, you will increase their performance and make them more accountable for behaving successfully.
- **Coaching** – These sessions are different from WIMs. Coaching is specific to a particular attitude, behavior, or technique that you want your employees to improve. Coaching can take place one-on-one or in a group, and is usually combined with role-play.
- **Touch calls** – Touch calls are quick reach-outs to current clients, or, if you manage employees who are geographically separate from you, employees. The purpose of these calls is to spend four or five minutes with a client or employee getting specific feedback about the performance of your company, or of you as a manager, and to set expectations for next steps around the feedback you uncover.
- **Recruiting interviews** – Effective sales leaders must always be recruiting! Even if you're not currently hiring, interviewing weekly helps you in two ways. First, you keep your interviewing skills sharp for when you really need to interview. Second, you establish "bench strength" for your team. That way, if an employee leaves unexpectedly, you can reach to your bench for a candidate instead of hiring the first person who "looks good." A supplemental benefit of interviewing weekly is that you may uncover a hidden gem

candidate you can add to your team immediately! Would you turn down a rock star candidate just because you didn't currently have an opening for that role? No! When you find truly great people, don't let them go. Even if it takes a while to bring them to your team, bring them onboard! One Sandler trainer I know has a three-year recruitment process for bringing salespeople into his organization.

Exercise – Your Cookbook

Create a cookbook for yourself for the next 90 days.

Today's Date:

_____

Deadline (90 days from today):

_____

Activity	Month Goal	Mon	Tues	Wed	Thurs	Fri	Sat	Sun	Total
Group accountability meetings									
Weekly Individual Meetings									
Role-play									
Coaching									
Touch calls									
Recruiting Interviews									

Creating a cookbook can be a fun task, but the time you spend on creating your cookbook will be wasted if you don't possess the discipline to hit your cookbook targets each month.

You must possess fanatical discipline for completing the behaviors that will cause you to reach your cookbook targets. For example, if your sales team's cookbook target is asking for 20 referrals in one month, then a fanatically disciplined team will actually make at least 20 quality referral requests each month, and record them all for discussion during your 90-day cookbook review. That's quality behavior.

Winners ask themselves, "Does it advance my business?" before starting every activity. Thus, blasting out 20 random emails to 20 random people in your contact list asking for a referral may bring results, but specific, targeted, quality referral requests will bring better, more consistent results.

Too much activity will cause burnout, and too little activity will cause failure. Create a cookbook that is balanced, and commit to the discipline of hitting the targets each month.

COOKBOOK ANY GOAL!

Athletes in time or distance-based sports, such as running, swimming, or cycling, understand how to translate cookbooks to personal goals — even though they might call their cookbook a "training schedule." What you call it doesn't really matter. What matters is your willingness to cookbook any goal. My clients have asked me to help them create mind, body, and financial cookbooks, and I've been happy to do so.

To cookbook any goal, start with the end result you want to achieve, stated in the present tense. For example: "I am at my ideal weight of X," "I am a graduate of the University of _____," or "I am free of unnecessary stress." Then break accomplishing that result into specific, measurable behaviors. You may need to adjust your cookbook tracking if your behaviors take place over more than one month, like taking a class at a local post-secondary institution.

Below is a sample of a cookbook for someone whose goal is, "I am free of unnecessary stress."

Activity	Month Goal	Mon	Tues	Wed	Thurs	Fri	Sat	Sun	Total
Plan my week at home	4								
Plan my week at work	4								
Exercise for 30 minutes	8								
Eat breakfast I prepared at home	28/29								
Eat lunch during workdays	21/22								
Meditate for 5 minutes	30/31								
Sleep through the night									
Stress level (1-10)									

From the cookbook we can surmise that this person previously felt out of control from the beginning of the week because he didn't make time to plan ahead (activities to "plan my week"), didn't exercise (activity to "exercise"), and had poor eating habits starting with either skipping breakfast or eating breakfast on the run and continuing with skipping lunch (activities to "eat breakfast prepared at home" and "eat lunch") — probably because he was "too busy." What would be interesting to ask this person, when he did eat lunch prior to creating this cookbook, is how often it was eaten at his desk in a rush.

A few more notes on this cookbook:

- Notice that the "plan" entries have a goal of four per month, or once per week. Especially for personal goal cookbooks, you should include an activity with a goal of once per week that you will do at the start of each week, whether that's Sunday or Monday for you. Checking off a behavior goal at the beginning of your week provides a quick win for your brain and a bit of extra motivation when you might not feel like achieving your cookbook targets that week.

- This person included two activities with no goal, "sleep through the night" and "stress level (1-10)." Including a goal for "sleep through the night" would be detrimental to this person because not sleeping through the night would put him close to failing to achieve his goal, which would cause additional stress. Because this person is probably journaling* as well — an activity Sandler recommends to everyone — he can analyze his cookbook for patterns of restless or tranquil nights, and then journal about what happened that *caused* that restful or fitful sleep.

- Cookbooks are moldable as to what you want to track specifically. For this person, tracking his perceived stress level on a 1-10 scale was important probably as another source for reflection in the journal.

---

* *A quick note on journaling. Journaling is one of the most critical, and often most ignored, suggestions Sandler trainers make to their clients. Many of the individuals we remember as "great" or "successful," from Abraham Lincoln to Marie Currie to Winston Churchill, all did some form of journaling. I journal every work day for two reasons. First, my journal helps me track my successes and failures so I can learn from both. Second, by writing down what happened to me that day, I can deal with any emotions related to those events so when someone asks me how my day was, I don't give him a bad day.*

Minimum Acceptable Performance (Map)

How often are one of these phrases heard in your company?

- "I'm not a micromanager."
- "I expect people to hit the ground running."
- "I hired them to..."
- "They know what they're supposed to do."

If our business world were a homogenous one, then those phrases would always be correct. *Every* sales job would be *exactly* like every other sales job, *every* expense filing procedure would be *exactly* the same at every company, and *every* role would have *exactly* the same weekly behavior expectations.

What these phrases actually do in our real world, however, is throw your new hires into the deep end of the pool, with ankle weights on, and an expectation of keeping their head above water with little or no help from you. Even if your company doesn't have a formal on-boarding plan, you can give new hires a better chance at swimming if you start them off with a MAP – a Minimal Acceptable Performance plan.

This is a set of written guidelines that clearly spells out the one to three behaviors that you expect new hires to complete *every* week, during their initial weeks with your company. You can think of this as an on-boarding process boiled down to one page.

When creating your MAP, remember: *Never manage the numbers, manage the behavior.* What that means, for a salesperson, is that the MAP *won't* include closed sales but it might include the number of cold calls completed, number of first appointments with prospects, or number of networking events attended.

For a MAP to be successful, the behavior(s) must be observable. "Knowing our product" isn't an observable behavior. "Number of presentations made" is. But making presentations isn't the focus of professional sales.

The MAPs you create will be slightly different depending on your expectations for a specific role and the skills a new hire brings to that role.

Being given a MAP provides two benefits for new hires:

- **They feel that you care about their success** – Multiple surveys have shown that the number one reason for employees leaving is that they felt their employer/manager didn't care about them.

- **It gives them an opportunity to get quick wins** – Quick wins reduce ramp-up time for salespeople, which means they become producers faster.

For you, the manager, a MAP provides three benefits:

- **You and your employee have a clear understanding, up front, of your performance expectations** – No more wasted time with "I didn't know I had to do that" conversations.

- **Leading indicators of success or failure** – If your new hire fails to stick to his MAP, you know *within weeks* instead of *months later* when his sales report shows a negative number, allowing you to make faster decisions about termination or additional training.

- **More productive one-on-one meetings** – Remember, as a manager your only asset is your time. Instead of spending 45 minutes going through your new hire's week, you have a 5-minute conversation about his MAP (which can extend to a longer period if either of you feel additional coaching or training is needed).

As an added advantage, you'll probably find, after implementing MAPs for all of your new hires, that you have more free time on your hands. Enjoy!

Exercise – Minimum Acceptable Performance

Write down a role in your organization, then write down the one to three behaviors you expect a new hire to complete in his initial weeks with the company.

Role:

_____

_____

Behaviors:

1._____

_____

2._____

_____

3._____

_____

The chief executives and owners we work with often give this exercise to their *current* employees after they define the MAP for each role. In their experience, what their existing employees write down as the MAP for their role and what their manager wrote down only matches up 33 percent of the time!

Think about that for a minute. If that data were true for your company, then 67 percent of the time your employees are working on tasks that *aren't* helping you advance your business!

Case in Point – Implementing MAP

A client of ours, a manufacturer's representative, implemented MAP during performance reviews one year. In the following twelve months the company had zero turnover, increased productivity, and spent less time directing its employees.

LET THEM CREATE THEIR COOKBOOK

Leaders are rope makers. It is their employees' choice to climb the rope or to hang themselves with it.

For a leader without a cookbook, holding the team accountable, coaching the team, and mentoring the team is a major challenge. For a leader with a cookbook, these tasks become considerably easier. But from where, ideally, should the cookbook come?

Human beings, as we have seen, are motivated by goals they choose for themselves as opposed to quotas imposed upon them. If you let your employees define their own mountaintops, it doesn't really make a lot of sense for you to then force them up a path of your own design.

Some leaders might say that it is their right as leaders to design an employee's path for him. From a literal definition of "leader" this may seem to make sense. Yet if you have ever spent any time around small children, you understand that forcing someone down a path that that person didn't design is much harder than walking alongside someone who just happened to choose to go in the direction you wanted.

Supporting your employees as they create their individual cookbooks means you must be vulnerable and trust that you hired the right individuals for the role they occupy in your organization. This exercise will also help you weed out any employees who might become resisters to your accountability program. Their cookbook will either have few specific, measurable behaviors with very low targets set, or will not materialize at all, because they will continually delay creating the cookbook with statements like, "I'm not sure what to do," or "Why are you micromanaging me?" Assuming such patterns persist over time, you don't want these people in your organization anyway.

The fact that we recommend each employee create his own cookbook does not mean that you as his manager can't include one or two *non-negotiables, need-to-haves,* and *nice-to-haves.* (See below.) Your challenge in getting your employees to incorporate these elements into their cookbook lies in making each of your items naturally integrate with the behaviors your employees would have come up with on their own.

Non-Negotiables

A non-negotiable, of course, is a behavior that must happen consistently. For example, we strongly recommend that it is non-negotiable for outside salespeople to include both "meetings booked" and "meetings held" as *separate* line items in their cook-book. Although these numbers should be tracked carefully, and separately, I have to point out that many of our clients have gotten good results by attaching *no* weekly or monthly numerical goal to either metric. This reduces the pressure and helps establish a collaborative dialogue about the behavior. Tracking the ratios of these figures can give you and your salespeople important data to discuss during your WIMs and coaching sessions.

Need-To-Haves

Need-to-haves typically fall under the category of pre-existing metrics. David Sandler once said: "I'm giving you sheet music; now you make it play in your world." If you have metrics in place for which your employees are already accountable, and you're getting good results, you can keep using those metrics. Don't tear down everything you've built just because you read this book. Take what you already have and overlay our accountability system, the sheet music, onto that.

One of our clients, a salesperson who decided to invest in herself by paying for coaching out of her own pocket, struggled at first with the task of making our sheet music sing when she was introduced to the concept of the cookbook. She had a pre-existing key performance indicator (KPI) of 15 face-to-face meetings per week with clients or prospects. Her struggles went away, however, when she integrated that KPI into her cookbook as a starting point for establishing her other cookbook behaviors.

Nice-To-Haves

Nice-to-haves are really just suggestions of things that you'd like to see your employees include in their cookbook. For new managers, for instance, "touch calls to clients" is a nice behavior to include in their cookbook. When you roll out your accountability program, your employees will look to you for guidance. Without giving them the answer for building their own cookbook, share some nice-to-haves with them that would naturally roll up to their need-to-haves and non-negotiables. Carrying on the salesperson example above, if a need-to-have was 15 face-to-face meetings per week, the nice-to-haves would be all of the prospecting methods, active and passive, that that salesperson would use to get in front of 15 decision makers per week.

Exercise – Non-Negotiable, Need-To-Have, Nice-To-Have

Write down the name of a specific department or team in your company.

What are the one or two *non-negotiables* that you want to see in the cookbook for each person in that department?

_____

_____

_____

_____

What are the one or two *need-to-haves* that you want to see in the cookbook for each person in that department?

_____

_____

_____

_____

What are the *nice-to-have* behaviors that a member of the team could do to get data to help track his need-to-haves and non-negotiables?

_____

_____

_____

_____

_____

_____

_____

_____

_____

_____

FOUR RULES FOR CREATING A GREAT COOKBOOK

When we coach our clients on creating cookbooks, we share the following four rules, which ensure successful implementation.

- **Set monthly goals, but track weekly** – A large part of the anxiety around cookbooks arise from questions such as, "What if I have an off week?" or "What if I'm on vacation?" By setting monthly goals you have the flexibility to catch up on your cookbook if your discipline slips for one week. By tracking weekly you have an early warning system that will alert you to a drop off in your behavior before a lack of behavior starts affecting lagging indicators.

- **Track your cookbook for 90 days before making changes** – Especially when creating a cookbook for the first time, changing it prior to 90 days means you probably don't have enough data to get a clear picture of your progress. Typically, the problem in the early days isn't behavior, it's self-doubt. At the very least you should review your cookbook every 90 days to ensure that behaviors and monthly targets are still advancing you toward the chosen goals. Six months after launching my Sandler business, I discovered during a cookbook review that my behaviors and targets were turning me into a telemarketer. I reduced the amount of activities that caused that problem and increased my targets for activities that would actually advance me toward my goals.

- **Once you hit your monthly target for a specific behavior, you can stop doing it** – When you hit your monthly target in a specific area, you can, if you wish, stop doing it and do another behavior that will advance you toward achieving your goals.

- **Include some behaviors with no target attached** – Tracking an occasional behavior with no specific target attached allows you to gain additional insights and discussion points.

Below is an example of both a cookbook template and a completed cookbook for an employee with variable compensation. We find that a personal financial goal is a greater motivator than a company target, as it's understood that hitting a personal financial goal typically coincides with meeting or exceeding the company target.

COOKBOOK FOR SUCCESS TEMPLATE

Today's Date:_____

Personal Financial Goal: _____

Deadline: _____

Activity	Month Goal	Mon	Tues	Wed	Thurs	Fri	Sat	Sun	Total

COOKBOOK FOR SUCCESS SAMPLE

Today's Date: April 1
Personal Financial Goal: $15,000 in commissions earned
Deadline: June 30

Activity	Month Goal	Mon	Tues	Wed	Thurs	Fri	Sat	Sun	Total
Prospecting calls	120								
Unique conversations with decision makers	60								
Networking events	8								
LinkedIn® introduction requests	12								
Introductions received									
Meetings booked									
Meetings held									

THIS CHAPTER IN 45 SECONDS

- High achievers understand that the fastest way for them to reach a mountaintop is to sketch out a path that defines the specific, measurable behaviors required.
- If you are struggling to achieve one or more of your goals, or have abandoned them all together, you may be caught in the procrastination triangle.
- Never manage your numbers. Manage your behavior.
- On average, lagging indicators don't give a true picture of

a business for three to six months, whereas leading indicators can provide a clear picture of the health of your business in just three to six weeks.

- Crucial numbers for you to define are the leading indicators — the inputs that will cause your lagging indicators to happen.
- If you have no leading indicators, start with a four-week behavior tracking study.
- A MAP, Minimum Acceptable Performance, is the one to three behaviors that you expect your new hire to complete *every* week during his initial weeks with your company.
- Leaders are rope makers. It is his employees' choice to climb the rope or hang themselves with it. For a leader without a cookbook, it is very challenging to hold his team accountable or to coach and mentor them.
- Just because your employees create their own cookbooks doesn't mean you can't request non-negotiables and need-to-haves and suggest nice-to-haves in their cookbook.
- Set monthly goals, but track weekly.
- Track your cookbook for 90 days before making changes.
- Include behaviors with no targets attached.
- Cookbook any goal by starting with the result you want to achieve and then breaking the steps required to reach that result into specific, measurable activities (behaviors).
- Include an activity in your cookbook with a weekly goal of "one" that you will complete at the beginning of the week to give yourself a quick win and extra motivation for reaching your other cookbook targets.
- Your leader/manager cookbook should focus on activities that develop your people.

CHAPTER FOUR

The Consequence Principle

I mplementation of the accountability system I've shared with you in the previous chapters depends upon a simple principle: Without consequences, accountability is meaningless.

Unfortunately, the dominant perception in the business world is that the word "consequences" automatically means, "You're fired." That's like launching a thermonuclear weapon in response to getting into a fender-bender on the highway!

Consequence simply means "the result or effect of an action or condition." There's no moral judgment here. It's just what happens as a result of something else happening — and consequences can be either positive or negative. Let's look at a couple of positive examples of consequences:

- A salesperson, Stan, chooses to make prospecting calls the afternoon of a Friday before a long weekend when some of his colleagues are headed out the door. **Positive consequence:** Stan finally reaches and books a meeting with one of his top prospects — someone he's attempted to contact for six months.

- Before going to bed, you choose to do the dishes so your spouse comes down to a clean kitchen tomorrow morning. **Positive consequence:** Improved relationship with your spouse.

By the same token, there are obviously negative consequences associated with consistently *failing* to take action in each of these areas! In the first case, Stan might miss his quota for the quarter. In the second case, you might experience a challenge with your spouse that you weren't expecting.

Notice that it takes a whole lot of failure to take action, in example one, to put Stan's job in jeopardy, and it takes a whole lot of failure, in example two, to initiate divorce proceedings. There are a many, many steps in between!

Here's a thought: Suppose you were to establish *intentional* consequences that came a step or two before, and even prevented, deeply unpleasant *unintentional* ones (like blowing quota or starting an epic fight with the person you love most).

As I have discussed in previous chapters, accountability starts with your goals — with the personal mountaintops that you want or need to climb. Next come the specific behaviors that you will perform on a weekly basis — your path to each mountaintop. Finally, your accountability plan includes the consequences you will face if you *don't* stick to your weekly behavior plan (your cookbook).

Two Types of Consequences

Effective consequences, whether personal or professional, always relate to one of two things: time or money.

As calendars become more and more tightly scheduled, we find that time consequences are, as a general rule, more powerful motivators than money consequences. One of the most important points to bear in mind here, however, is that the consequence that motivates you is not necessarily the consequence that moves your direct reports. Your challenge as a manager is to understand which type of consequence will motivate each individual on your team.

Case in Point — Consequence Case Study

The Managing Partner of a major financial services company called me in to help him figure out how to motivate one of his sales salespeople. Let's call that employee Salesperson A. Salesperson A had all of the "surface level" traits of Salesperson B, who was a top performer — but Salesperson A consistently took Fridays off and came in late on Mondays, especially between September and December.

After sitting down with both salespeople individually we came to understand that Salesperson A was indeed highly motivated — to go hunting — while Salesperson B was highly motivated to maximize his bonus. During our debrief, the Managing Partner had an "Aha!" moment. Salesperson A could be just as productive as Salesperson B, if Salesperson A faced time consequences instead of money consequences. That was the best way of holding Salesperson A accountable to his cookbook! This change led to a breakthrough in sales productivity for Salesperson A. Even though Salesperson A and Salesperson B had very similar sales styles, these two people were motivated by very different consequences.

FOCUS CONSEQUENCES ON PERFORMANCE, NOT PEOPLE (I/R THEORY)

Another reason managers struggle with implementing consequences as part of an accountability program is the perception that consequences say "You are a bad person" to employees.

David Sandler discovered that salespeople tend to be most effective when they feel OK about themselves. The "Identity/Role" or "I/R" Theory he developed can help managers do a better job of coaching — by keeping employees OK while holding them accountable.

WHAT IS I/R THEORY?

Sandler's now-famous I/R Theory states that you can only perform in your roles in a manner consistent with how you see yourself conceptually. Your "Identity" is your own sense of self-worth as a person. Your "Role" side, by contrast, connects to all of the roles or labels you apply, or have applied, to things you *do*.

Represented visually, the I/R chart might look like this:

I	**R**
• Self-esteem • Self-worth • Self-image • Self-concept • Self-identity	• Spouse/Partner • Parent • Child • Sibling • Employer • Employee • Athlete • Writer • Cook • Singer • Artist • Traveler

Check Yourself

Here's an interesting exercise I'd like you to do. Using the I/R Theory diagram below, write down any labels you apply to yourself under the "R" side. Most people get at least 12. Don't proceed with the rest of the chapter until you've done this.

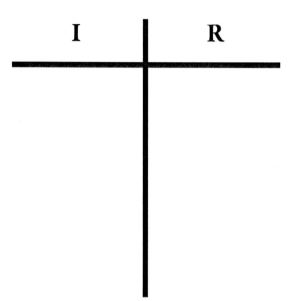

Now I want you to close your eyes and imagine that you are sitting comfortably alone — in your happy place. That could be your couch at home, or a warm beach, or a spot right next to a crackling fireplace at a ski lodge. Wherever it is, you are comfortable and alone, but you won't be alone long. With your eyes closed, I want you to imagine that for the next 15 minutes your "R" side is completely separate from your "I" side. None of the labels you wrote down apply to you for the next 15 minutes. All you have are your self-worth, your self-concept, your self-identity, your self-image, and your self-esteem. Take a deep breath in, let it out slowly and then open your eyes.

Now I want you to write down a number on the "I" side from 1-10, where "1" is low and "10" is high, to describe how you feel with no labels applied.

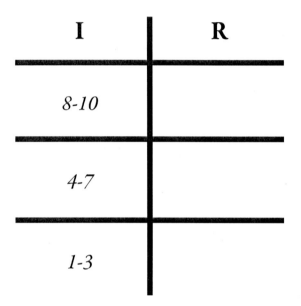

I/R Theory is critical for implementing accountability and consequence programs. How you view yourself conceptually (just your "I" side) will be a strong indicator of how you will react to accountability and consequences.

You'll notice that the I/R Theory diagram above is split into three parts. Under the "R" side next to 8-10 write "winner," next to 4-7 write "at-leaster," and next to 1-3 write "non-winner."

Applying I/R Theory to Consequences

So how does all this apply to consequences? Let's take a look at the typical behaviors of each group.

- **Winners** – Winners take responsibility for their actions. They tend to internalize failure (in a good way). That means they understand David Sandler's rule, "There are no bad prospects, only bad salespeople." For example, a salesperson who is told by a CEO that he is delegating to his VP of sales, and that the VP of sales is the final decision maker, will blame himself for not asking the CEO what kind of budget approval authority his VP of sales has. In other words, if the VP of sales reveals that he can't approve expenditures of more than a few thousand dollars, and that comes as a surprise to the salesperson, that's on the salesperson — nobody else.

  Winners like accountability programs. Why? Because those programs provide an unambiguous method for a winner to demonstrate success. Winners *appreciate* consequences because winners take responsibility for their actions and understand that consequences follow failure.

- **At-Leasters** – At-Leasters say things like, "I did my best; at least I tried." They aren't the best, but "at-least" they aren't the worst. In my experience, *at-leasters dislike accountability programs* because, under such programs, the ability to make excuses about performance is taken away. At-Leasters may cry "micro-management" when an accountability program is implemented. At-leasters *fear* consequences because they may see consequences as a personal attack.

- **Non-Winners** – This label does not pass judgment on anyone; it describes a psychological position that people can and do change. Those who occupy the Non-Winner psychological position do not take responsibility for their actions or outcomes. They tend to externalize their failures by blaming outside forces and events for what happens in their lives. Some people in this category develop a "Why even try?" attitude. *Many people in this category don't even understand accountability programs* because they don't believe they themselves control the outcomes of their actions. Regarding an accountability program, someone in the Non-Winner psychological position might say, *"What does it matter what I do anyway?"* *Non-Winner may accept consequences,* but usually are not motivated by them because they feel they have no control over their lives anyway. For them, consequences generally fall into the "Why does this always happen to me?" column.

"I Am an I-10"

Before you move on, find a separate piece of paper. Write on that sheet, or write down in the margins of this book, this phrase: "I am an I-10."

It doesn't matter what you wrote down in the earlier exercise, and you shouldn't try to go back and change your score. To successfully implement accountability and consequences, you *must* believe in your heart that you are an I-10.

Being an I-10 doesn't mean you are perfect, and it doesn't mean that you don't have "head trash" that can hold you back from peak performance. We all have head trash. Being an I-10 just means that you separate success in your roles from your value as a person. It means that you see failure as a learning opportunity instead of a judgment on your self-worth.

As a leader, your aim should be to internalize the "I am an I-10" mantra and use I/R Theory as a lens to evaluate your employees' behavior and help them become happier, more productive, and willing participants in your accountability program.

Exercise – I/R Theory and Your Team

Using the I/R diagram below, write the first names of each member of your team in the "winner," "at-leaster," and "non-winner" sections by guessing how each of them would score themselves on their "I" side if they did the "happy place" exercise at the beginning of this chapter.

The purpose of this exercise is to help you figure out who will be your champions (winners) and resisters (at-leasters) when you implement your accountability program. You are not judging your team members' worth as human beings.

Be critical when you think of each person. An interesting exercise would be for you to do the "happy place" exercise with your team at your next meeting to find out how close your scores match theirs.

I	R
8-10 *Winner*	
4-7 *At-Leaster*	
1-3 *Non-Winner*	

I/R Theory in Action

The "You're fired" consequence is usually taken as a personal attack, even if it's only implied indirectly — or perceived without the manager even meaning to move toward that consequence! Here's how most salespeople translate/escalate that consequence, even when they didn't even mean to send that message: *"You" failed, so "you" are a bad person.*

Actually the "You're fired" signal (when it's sent) is really about role performance. It means: *"You" failed in this role so "you" are no longer employed by this company.*

Keeping an employee "OK" while discussing poor role performance is one of your greatest challenges as a manager. Let's look at two scenarios to understand how this conversation might go. In each scenario, the manager discusses poor performance with a marketing person who has consistently failed to meet deadlines on the redesign of the company's new Web site.

Scenario one:

Manager: Help me understand how you keep missing deadlines. Our new site should have been live at the end of last month and, based on what you just told me, we might not have it up until after our busy season. Why do you keep missing the mark?

Marketer: It's just that I keep getting more stuff piled on my desk. A week after the Web project was finalized you gave me the new product launch on which to work.

Manager: I appreciate that, but we need to get our new site up before busy season. I'm getting heat from upstairs. If you work late all of next week you should be able to get it done.

Marketer: Sure, I guess I can do that.

Scenario two:

Manager: Help me understand how these deadlines were missed. My understanding was we were going to be live at the end of last month.

Marketer: It's just that I keep getting more stuff piled on my desk. A week after the Web project was finalized you gave me the new product launch on which to work.

Manager: Thank you for refreshing my memory. If I remember correctly we sat down to discuss your cookbook when I gave you the new product launch. What do you remember about that meeting?

Marketer: I said that I could fit in both if I could give away the other project on which I was working.

Manager: And?

Marketer: And you took that other project off my plate.

Manager: Do you remember what we agreed to if you didn't finish the Web project on time?

Marketer: I said that I would work evenings and weekends until it was done.

Manager: So what do you want to do about this?

Marketer: I'll come in this weekend. I should have enough time to get you a final draft for Monday morning.

Manager: OK. What, if anything should I do if I don't have the final draft on Monday morning?

Marketer: I'll let you know Sunday night where I'm at and if I need to come in early on Monday to finish up.

Manager: Works for me. How can I help you?

Marketer: I've got it. Thanks.

In the first scenario, the manager made this issue all about the employee as a person ("Why do *you* keep missing the mark?"). That attacks the employee's "I" side and breaks trust between the manager and his employee. When that happens, people go into "fight or flight" mode. Because employees can't, as a general rule, literally flee, or physically attack you, "flight" becomes "excuse making."

Notice that the manager also *imposed* the consequences on the employee (work late all of next week) instead of letting the employee determine the consequences. If we fast-forward to the end of the following week in scenario one we can expect that the same conversation will happen again!

In the second scenario, however, the manager kept the focus on role performance ("these deadlines"), and when the employee threw out an excuse, he responded with a question instead of getting equally defensive. To get the employee back on track, this manager referred back to previous commitments and helped to set a new up-front contract, complete with new mutually acceptable consequences should the employee fail to perform again. Both manager and employee leave this scenario feeling OK, and the employee feels valued, which increases trust in his manager.

Here's an open secret about human beings: *We tend to be motivated to perform if we feel we have some choice in both how we will complete a task and the consequences for failing.*

As a result, the employee in the second scenario is likely to be more motivated than the employee in the first scenario. If we fast-forward the second scenario, we can expect the manager to see a final draft of the new Web site on Monday morning.

Tailoring Consequences to Each Employee

Looking back at that story I shared with you involving Salesperson A and Salesperson B from a little earlier in this chapter, we can see that each employee was motivated by profoundly different factors. Addressing this reality is known as "situational management." Instead of implementing consequences to a supposedly homogeneous whole, you tailor consequences for each department or member of your team.

That sounds like more work, but in fact it's not. That "extra work" happens up front instead of after the fact. It's usually far less work than firing someone and securing a suitable replacement!

Benefits of "Situational" Management

Traditional management implements accountability and consequences to the entire group instead of tailoring consequences to each member of the team. This makes about as much sense as putting pole-vaulters, shot-putters, and sprinters on the same weight-lifting plan.

Traditional management spends a lot of time managing the accountability program "after the fact," fighting fires, and dealing with "special situations."

Because situational management starts with an understanding of each team member's goals, the cookbook for each goal's accountability and consequences is specific to each person on his team, while still driving toward an overall team goal.

Situational management spends a lot of time setting up a sandbox in which the team can play. It then sits back and lets the team play, only getting involved when a team member strays outside the sandbox. It's much, much easier than traditional management!

LET YOUR EMPLOYEES CHOOSE THEIR STICK

In our experience the most successful consequences are those set up by employees themselves.

Initially employees will resist helping you set up consequences because they expect there's going to be some dire outcome. The trick is to help employees understand that you are only having the conversation so that you *never* have to use the consequences to which you agree. Once that much is clear, you will generally find that they will open up and your conversation will be more productive.

By the way, it's best to have this conversation offsite, and to give each person involved at least a few days' notice that one of your agenda topics will be consequences of failing to complete their cookbooks each week. This prevents outside distractions and helps your team come prepared with thoughtful responses. "Springing it" on your team members may leave people feeling trapped and create unhelpful on-the-spot reactions when you ask for consequences.

EXAMPLES OF CONSEQUENCE PROGRAMS

Following are three consequence programs relating to different roles. Keep in mind that these programs only take effect if an employee *doesn't do* the behaviors in his cookbook for that week. Think of a consequence program as a ladder that you can move up, down, or off completely, depending on performance.

CO-CREATED CONSEQUENCES FOR THREE DIFFERENT PEOPLE / THREE DIFFERENT ROLES

Role – Salesperson (*Employee X*)	Role – Outbound Customer Service Specialist (*Employee Y*)	Role – Marketing Specialist (*Employee Z*)
• First offense – Make up numbers by end of following week. • Second offense – Verbal warning. • Third offense – Written warning. • Fourth offense – $X deducted from next paycheck to reflect company's investment in his mobile phone bill. • Fifth offense – Second written warning. • Sixth offense – Termination.	• First offense – Verbal warning. • Second offense – Written warning. • Third offense – Work an extra shift before the end of the month. • Fourth offense – Second written warning. • Fifth offense – Termination.	• First offense – Stay late/work weekend to complete project by deadline. • Second offense – Verbal warning. • Third offense – Written warning. • Fourth offense – Work shift answering phones. • Fifth offense – Second written warning. • Sixth offense – Termination.

Notice that termination only arises upon the sixth (noticed!) offense! That seems like a lot of second chances, doesn't it? That's intentional. Notice, too, that each and every benchmark is created during a collaborative discussion with the employee.

Keep in mind, too, that accountability is a *weekly* process, so a salesperson, for instance, could theoretically move from first offense to sixth offense and termination in less than two months. That's pretty quick. Considering the cost to hire, on-board, and terminate an underperforming employee, which is estimated at somewhere between 4.5 and 6.2 times his salary, a *co-created* consequence program allows you to quickly terminate someone who just isn't working out, which saves time, money, and morale.

Case in Point – Accountability Reduces Turnover

Often, the biggest managerial fear when it comes to implementing an accountability program that includes consequences is the perceived pain of firing and recruiting. One of my clients, who was highly resistant to putting in an accountability program with actual consequences, implemented a program for his sales team very similar to the one described a moment ago. He ended up losing only two people. The worst performer on the team resigned. This was a low-performing player who worked his way through the consequence program in about three months, and was then let go. Now comes the moral of the story: After that, the company had *no* issues with turnover, and the sales team performed better — because everyone knew the specific behaviors to which they were being held accountable! Of course, everyone also knew the consequences for not performing. *If there are never any consequences to anyone for not being accountable, the accountability program will not work.*

No Mutual Mystification

You don't want to focus only on the negatives, of course. It's just as important to discuss with your team how someone gets *out of* the consequence program. For example, if someone fails to meet his cookbook targets one week, but makes them up the following week, does he get to go back to "zero" on the consequence ladder, or does he need to maintain performance for a specific number of weeks before moving back down? Everybody needs to understand — and buy into — the rules by which your team operates. There are many variations on these discussions. For instance: Can someone go from level four consequences to zero if he meets his cookbook targets for a specific number of weeks? You must collaboratively work with your team to set up these guidelines — and then you must stand behind them.

There must be no "mutual mystification" between you and your employees. Just as accountability can't exist without consequences, accountability can't exist with ambiguity!

DEALING WITH "SPECIAL" SITUATIONS

Whenever an accountability program is implemented for a group of employees, some people will attempt to wear you down by asking you to deal with a host of "special" situations. For instance:

- What happens if I don't hit my cookbook targets because I'm on vacation?
- What happens if I hit my revenue/project goals, but don't reach the targets in my cookbook?
- What happens if I have to deal with a bunch of client issues so I don't have time to do the behaviors in my cookbook?
- What happens if operations doesn't deliver on time?
- What happens if I hit my targets, but the rest of the team doesn't?

Those are the most common "What if" scenarios, and you are well advised to prepare for them ahead of time. The end goal of this group is to make you give them just enough wiggle room for them to justify not following your accountability program. For your accountability program to be successful, you really must have fanatical discipline when it comes to inspiring people to stay focused and hit the cookbook targets daily, weekly, and monthly. Initially, creating this kind of focus takes a lot of work, but it's the only known way to support someone who is in the process of transforming from an at-leaster into a winner.

Remember that we are talking about collaboration here. The fact that you ask your employees to come up with their own proposals for their consequences does not mean that you will just rubber stamp each proposal. As their manager, you are well within your rights to push back, gently, on suggestions if you feel they are going too easy or aren't taking the exercise seriously.

IMPLEMENT ACCOUNTABILITY WITH CONSEQUENCES

Once you and your team agree to the consequence ladder, everyone should know how someone moves down the ladder and how someone moves off the ladder. This gives us, perhaps, an opportunity for the ultimate up-front contract between manager and employee.

Up-front contracts for implementing accountability and consequence programs take many forms. Here is one example:

	Accountability Up-Front Contract
	<ul><li>Purpose (reason for program).</li><li>The employee's cookbook and consequences.</li><li>Your approval of his cookbook and consequences.</li><li>Check-in (how often: weekly, or monthly).</li><li>Consequence ladder (how employees get on and move up, down, or off).</li></ul>

Besides having each employee sign off on his consequence ladder, you should also post consequences wherever your employees' cookbooks live — either on a public "big board" or within your CRM system.

Accountability programs only succeed with transparency and clearly defined metrics that connect to both performance and consequences.

News flash: It goes both ways! Successful implementation of an accountability program also requires *you* to have your own set of consequences for not meeting *your* cookbook obligations each week. And if you are serious about winning buy-in to this program, you will let your employees help you create *your* consequences. This makes you vulnerable to them. Remember, vulnerability is a key trait of successful leaders. Being vulnerable in the accountability process makes your employees more likely to keep their commitments to you.

WHAT DOES A LEADER'S CONSEQUENCE LADDER LOOK LIKE?

As for your own consequence ladder, you should try to keep your consequences positive. As a leader your time is probably already stretched thin, so consequences like, "I'll work late" (you probably are already) or "I won't go to the gym at noon next week" (you probably aren't already) only reinforce work/life balance problems. In addition, be sure that a consequence like, "I'll throw the team a pizza party" doesn't cause your employees to sabotage your own cookbook with regard to, say, pizza consumption. A positive consequence might be "I get a day off."

If it happens that you get on your own consequence ladder, be open about it. Public demonstrations of accountability to your employees show them that accountability isn't just a "flavor of the month" program.

Exercise – Your Consequence Ladder

If I don't hit my cookbook targets each week my consequence ladder will be:

1. _____

_____

_____

2. _____

_____

_____

3. _____

_____

_____

4. _____

_____

_____

5. _____

_____

_____

6. _____

_____

_____

COMMITMENT TO IMPLEMENTING AN ACCOUNTABILITY PROGRAM

I, _____, hereby commit to holding a meeting with my team where we will co-create an accountability program and related consequences by (date) _____.

CONSEQUENCES FOR ONE

As a business owner or commission-only salesperson, you basically report to yourself. But that doesn't mean you can't implement consequences!

For you, consequences will be a series of "if-then" statements. For example, "If I don't hit my 'referral request' target for the week, then I can't take Friday afternoon off to train for my marathon."

When implementing a consequence program for one person, it is critical that you recruit an accountability partner who has permission to hold you accountable to your cookbook. The benefit of an accountability partner program is that you hold each other accountable — so you each have an incentive to excel.

It's best if your accountability partner isn't someone with whom you have a strong emotional attachment like your spouse or partner. From personal experience, spouses and partners tend to have difficulty holding each other accountable because resentment can grow when punishments are applied.

WHAT HAPPENS IF YOU IGNORE THIS CHAPTER?

Failing to implement consequences with your team means that your accountability program will become just one more time-sinkhole for you to deal with each week. Why bother? By co-creating consequences with your team instead of imposing those

consequences on your own, you will make your team more engaged, more productive, and less likely to need the consequences
you created.

THIS CHAPTER IN 45 SECONDS

- Without consequences, accountability can't exist.
- Consequences can be positive or negative. Negative consequences usually result from *failing* to take action.
- Effective consequences are based on either time or
  money. As our lives become overscheduled, time consequences tend to be the most useful for holding employees accountable.
- I/R Theory separates our value as a person ("I" side) from
  the labels we apply to ourselves ("R" side). We will perform
  in a comfort zone on our "R" side corresponding to how
  we score ourselves on our "I" side.
- "I" side "winners" take responsibility for their actions and
  welcome both accountability and consequence programs.
  I-side "at-leasters" dislike accountability programs because,
  under such programs, the ability to make excuses about
  performance is taken away, and may see consequences as a
  personal attack. "I" side "losers" externalize their failures.
- When discussing consequences, focus on an employee's
  performance ("R" side) instead of his self-worth ("I" side).
- Tailor consequences to each employee.
- Co-create a "consequence ladder" with your employees
  and mutually agree to the rule for how someone gets on
  and how they move up, down, or off.
- Consequences will create turnover, but will also result in
  greater productivity.

- Consequences for one are both viable and necessary. Find an accountability buddy, not your spouse or partner, who has permission to mete out rewards and punishments.

CHAPTER FIVE

Implementing the Accountability Program

Successfully implementing an accountability program is no easy matter. It boasts not one, but four, starting points.

First, start with yourself. You're their leader. That means you need to be an inspirational model for your employees by exhibiting discipline and adhering to your own accountability plan.

Second, start clearly with an up-front contract to which everyone agrees. Let me emphasize that word *clearly*. With apologies to the founding fathers of Las Vegas, I point out that *what happens in vagueness, stays in vagueness.*

Third, start strong by sticking to the consequence ladder, even when you don't feel like it. Your employees will test your commitment by testing your resolve to levy consequences.

Fourth, start from day one by building an accountability program into your on-boarding plan.

Get a clean start on each of those four steps and you should have a smooth implementation.

START WITH YOU (THEIR LEADER)

By now you know that implementing a successful accountability program starts with you, the leader. You must set the example for accountability and be the model for behavior. If you aren't personally willing to be held accountable, your entire program is doomed. It's that simple.

Recall that in Sandler's Success Triangle one of the key elements of success is discipline. I define discipline as "keeping appointments with yourself." If something is important enough for you to schedule in your calendar, it's important enough for you to actually do! Start by reviewing your own calendar for the past week or month and note how many appointments with yourself (e.g. exercise, spent time with family, turned off smartphone, journaling, meditation) you kept, as compared with how many you didn't keep.

Exercise – How Disciplined Are You as Their Leader?

Review your calendar for the past week or month. How many "appointments with yourself" did you:

Keep _____   Miss _____

Based on what you learned, on a scale of 1-10, how would you rank your own discipline ("1" is low, "10" is high)? _____

If you scored low, that's not unusual. Often, the first person we start slipping with when it comes to accountability is ourselves.

A word of warning is in order, however. If you honestly would have scored yourself "zero" because you don't *have* any appointments to yourself in your calendar, let's forget about implementing an accountability program for your company, and implement and accountability program for you for the next two months so you can get a sense of the challenges and victories your employees will have when you roll a program out to them.

THE THREE WITHOUTS

1. Without discipline there can be no accountability.
2. Without accountability there can be no discipline.
3. Without consequences there can be neither.

Implementing your personal accountability program means setting up reasonable consequences, which are the foundation for your personal accountabilities and support your personal discipline to achieve your accountabilities.

ALL OR NOTHING?

Most people make two mistakes when they attempt to improve their discipline. They either attempt to go completely cold turkey, trying to change everything overnight, or they set the bar so low that they don't really have to do much of anything in order to change.

If you tend to fall in the completely cold turkey camp, you're probably already familiar with the various ways your mind and body undermine your attempts to improve your discipline. For example, let's say you decide that you're going to start waking up one hour earlier every morning and go for a run. That sounds great ... until your alarm goes off on the third day after you start your exercise accountability program. You're sore and it's raining outside and you're so warm under your covers... You've either experienced this personally or you have a friend who has, and you know how this story ends.

Instead of attempting to go completely cold turkey try making small, incremental adjustments to your routine. These are more difficult for your mind and/or body to resist. Using the example above, instead of committing to getting up one hour earlier and going for a run, get up six minutes earlier and do jumping jacks for one minute. For the first week you'll probably feel like you've exercised, and as your body adjusts to your new routine, you can set your clock back another six minutes and add another minute of exercise. Ten sets of "move your clock back," and you're at one hour.

BAR TOO LOW?

The "set the bar low" crowd are the opposite of the cold turkey crowd. Instead of dramatic personal change, they "commit" to personal changes so intangible they have no meaning. For example, "I'll smile more," "I'll think happier thoughts," or "I won't take my family for granted." These are all great concepts, but they are difficult to measure and they don't require any real effort or result in any mental calories being burned.

People fear change, so they'll often pay lip service to changing instead of actually committing to meaningful change and taking a disciplined approach to making that change.

For someone who falls into the "set the bar low" camp, successfully implementing an accountability program starts with committing to a small, tangible behavioral change for a couple of weeks. Then it's time to take that change one small step further for another two weeks until the "new" behavior becomes a habit.

For example, thousands of words have been written on the

benefits of meditation for people who consider themselves "busy." Yet the word "meditation" itself can create stress and anxiety because meditation has typically been interpreted as meaning "sitting without doing anything" for a period of 10 to 60-plus minutes, which a busy person can't imagine fitting into a highly scheduled day. It should be possible, though, to schedule *one* minute of meditation into your day, which can be nothing more than closing your eyes and counting to 60 slowly (one-one-thousand, two-one-thousand...)

After two weeks of one-minute meditation, you increase to ninety seconds, or two minutes if you're feeling brave, and you have a go for another two weeks. You increase slowly until you reach your desired minutes of meditation per day goal. My own experience is that five minutes is a good amount of daily meditation to refresh and clear my mind for the next tasks on my "to-do" list. Just as with the cold turkey situation, we want a situation where we buy into, and hold onto, increments of gradual positive change.

Changing your attitude towards an activity doesn't mean repeating "I love it, I love it, I love it," ("it" being the activity) over and over until your attitude changes. Our brains aren't built that way. Instead, pick a *behavior* that relates to the activity you don't like, set a small accountability goal for yourself, have the discipline to do the behavior, evaluate after two weeks, and then increase your behavior target and repeat for another two weeks. Over 12 weeks you should notice a slight softening in your attitude towards the activity, but you will probably never totally enjoy it. As David Sandler once said about a behavior that salespeople the world over are often tempted to avoid, "You don't have to *like* prospecting; you just have to do it."

Exercise – Committing to One Small Change

For the next two weeks I commit to _____

_____. My goal is_____ (number of minutes, repetitions, miles, etc.). I will start on (date) _____ and evaluate on (date) _____.

No matter how high or low you scored yourself on the discipline exercise earlier in this chapter, before you roll out an accountability program to your team or company, do the two-week change challenge. We mentioned at the beginning of this chapter that "the lead dog sets the pace." If you are already following a personal accountability plan before you roll out accountability company-wide, then you show your employees that accountability isn't a flavor of the month program that will quietly disappear.

Start Clearly: Up-Front Contracts

I can't overemphasize the importance of setting and abiding by up-front contracts. If your accountability program rolls out without all parties clearly understanding what they are personally accountable for weekly and monthly, how their accountability behaviors will be tracked and measured, the consequences for failing to meet their personal accountability behaviors, the purpose of the program, and the benefits of accountability, you can expect to spend a lot of time fighting fires and managing those special situations we covered a little earlier in the book.

One of David Sandler's rules was "No mind reading." That means both sides really and truly understand what's going on and what the expectations are. It is our responsibility as leaders to provide clarity *and* then test our assumptions about our employees' understanding of, and commitment to, the accountability program.

Here's a quick test of your ability to provide clarity to your employees. After you explain a new initiative or delegate a task to them, ask them to repeat back exactly what you expect them to do, when you expect them to deliver results, and what steps you expect them to take if they need help. If what comes out of their mouth doesn't match what's in your head, you have just received a great gift. You can fix the ambiguity between you and your employees before they have a chance to act on their misinterpretation of your request!

A key part of an up-front contract is that there is *mutual* agreement between all parties involved. An up-front contract doesn't exist if the terms are imposed on another person.

Below are two examples of how people try to establish up-front contracts:

You: We are launching an accountability program. You will create a plan for hitting your monthly goals and submit to your manager for approval. Your manager will check-in with you weekly to track your progress — these meetings have been entered into your calendar for you. We created a series of escalating consequences in case you don't reach your monthly goals. Thank you. Go about your business.

Or:

You: We will launch a program that will help both you and our company grow together. For that we need your help. In the next two weeks you will meet with your manager and your team to create specific behavior plans for accomplishing your monthly goals. You and your manager will also agree to a regular check-in schedule to make sure you are hitting your goals and you get the help you need to hit your goals. Those meetings may be less than five minutes. Part of our program includes an escalating series of consequences on the off chance that you miss your goals. You and your manager will co-create these consequences in the meeting I just mentioned. Once you and your manager agree to your behavior plan and consequences, both of you will sign off and implement your plan immediately. Are you OK with what I just described?

While wordier than the first example, the second up-front contract makes your employees feel that they have some control of the program. (In fact, the first example isn't an up-front contract at all. It's an ultimatum.) Ask for agreement to the terms of the up-front contract up front, so you have an opportunity to deal with any challenges or disagreements before starting implementation.

Let's look at each of the components of an implementation up-front contract in detail.

PURPOSE OF THE PROGRAM

The purpose of an accountability program is not to give "Big Brother" managers another stick with which to beat their teams. Accountability programs are supposed to create self-sufficiency and provide clear paths for growth and development.

To take your company to the next level, whatever that level is, you need your employees operating at 100 percent efficiency. In any business with more than a few employees, there are the top 20 percent, who may or may not be operating at 100 percent efficiency; the bottom 20 percent who are either so new they are still figuring out where the bathrooms are, or who you hope will go be successful elsewhere; and the middle 60 percent, who are trying to figure out how to move up to the top 20 percent.

Accountability programs create efficiency through self-sufficiency. Each person in the company understands what specific behaviors he needs to accomplish on a weekly or monthly basis. The "I'm not sure what to do" excuse goes away because the program is clearly stated and explicit in its terms — and because each person co-creates and signs off on a unique, personalized accountability plan!

Because successful accountability programs are clearly stated and explicit, there is clarity in how a participant follows the program. The middle 60 percent of your organization wants to be in the top 20 percent, but it's possible that, prior to your rolling out this program, they never got a road map that showed them how to get there. An accountability program provides them with that map.

THE FINANCIAL EFFECT OF HIGHER EFFICIENCY

If you could get the middle 60 percent of your organization to be just 10 percent more efficient, the positive financial impact to your business would be — well, you know that number better than I do. Is that number worth caring about? Is it worth sharing best practices that help the people in the middle 60 percent of your team up their game?

A quick note is in order here on the subject of privacy. Because each person creates his own accountability behavior plan, there may be some reluctance to share the plans of the top 20 percent, or the behaviors that individuals in each department do monthly. There are two responses to this reluctance.

First, sharing just the behaviors and not the specific behavior target shouldn't be a privacy concern because that is information that is shared with employees, both prospective and current, when they apply for a job with your organization. If one of your operations employees wants to switch to accounting, for instance, you would be doing him a disservice and retarding his personal and professional development if you didn't share with him what specific behaviors were required to work in accounting.

Second, I have to point out that, when it comes to management, "privacy" is sometimes a mask for "If they know what I do, they will think less of me." This is rarely ever true. One of our clients is the VP of sales for a telecommunications company in the eastern United States. Each quarter he posted, on the company intranet, not only his personal and professional goals, but also his specific accountability behavior plan for achieving each goal. He asked his team to hold him accountable to his behaviors. Our client consistently hit those goals and set the pace for accountability within the team.

Exercise – Privacy

The top reasons I wouldn't want to share my goals or accountability behavior plan with my team are:

_____

_____

_____

_____

_____

If my team knew about my goals and behavior plan and held me accountable, the positive impacts on my business would be:

_____

_____

_____

_____

Do the potential positive benefits outweigh your answers to the first question? If not, you'll have more work to do on your own attitudes toward accountability before you can successfully implement an accountability program in your organization.

Exercise – Purpose of Your Accountability Program (Why)

The purpose (why) of my accountability program is:

_____

_____

_____

_____

_____

_____

THEIR COOKBOOK AND CONSEQUENCES

At first glance, it might seem that having each employee create his own accountability behavior plan (cookbook) would be a massive waste of his time, as well as a waste of your time to review and approve. Consider, though, how hard you would have to swim if you created a standardized cookbook for each department and role within each department, and then tried to sell each person on using "your" cookbook.

The boss telling someone that he has to write five blog posts per week produces a significantly different motivation than an employee creating a cookbook that includes five blog posts per week, which is approved by his manager. Employees who create their own cookbooks tend to feel more engaged with their work and tend to exceed their cookbook targets regularly.

YOUR APPROVAL OF THEIR COOKBOOK AND CONSEQUENCES

When you ask an employee to create a cookbook that you will approve, there is an implicit agreement that you will keep him safe when he brings you what he created.

Don't be like the sales manager who, during role-plays, always plays the prospect from hell. If you throw the cookbook your employee created back in his face, you will break the bond of trust. Despite Machiavelli's famous declaration that it is better to be feared than loved, recent research, mostly by social psychologist Amy Cuddy, shows that, for a leader, it really is better to be loved than feared.

When you set your implementation up-front contract with your employees, tell them that you reserve the right to ask for revisions to their cookbook before you approve it. Then, if you spot potential problems, ask for help in resolving them.

Case in Point – Cookbook Approval the Right Way

We implemented cookbooks with an oilfield service company. Instead of having his salespeople go away and come back with a draft cookbook, the CEO set the expectation up front that during the meeting his salespeople would draft, submit, revise, and get approval for their cookbooks before they left for the day.

No surprise. There were a few salespeople who took creating their cookbooks seriously, a couple that went through the motions, and a couple who were outwardly hostile to the idea of accountability in the first place.

When each salesperson brought a draft cookbook in to the CEO, he took a moment to read it through, made sure the non-negotiables and need-to-haves were included, and then instead of making demands to include a specific behavior, increase the goal of a behavior, or take out a behavior altogether he asked a very pointed series of questions.

The questions sounded like this:

- Help me understand...
    - How this behavior will get you to your goals?
    - Why you chose this goal for this behavior?

- When you expect to fit all of this in/around your travel schedule?
- What do you want me to do if you don't reach these goals after one month? Two months?
- Why you would expect me to apply that consequence in that time frame?
- How committed you are to helping this company succeed?

The CEO's tonality was even more important than his words. When he asked his salespeople those questions his tone was nurturing and curious.

Because the CEO's tone suggested that he was seeking to help his salespeople instead of practicing "gotcha" management, the salespeople never felt like they were walking into a trap.

At the end of the series of meetings each salesperson, even the ones who were hostile to the idea of accountability at the beginning, had an approved cookbook. Everyone understood the consequences of not reaching his goals.

Within three weeks of that meeting, both of the salespeople who were hostile to the entire program left the company. This gave the CEO more time in his day, as he no longer had to fight them or the fires they brought.

CHECK-IN – WEEKLY OR MONTHLY

My recommendation, as you know by now, is to set monthly goals and manage them weekly. I emphasize the point now, as we're talking about implementation because it's the opposite of what most companies do. Most companies tend to rely on lagging indicators (sales closed, revenue, profit, jobs booked, work in progress, inventory turns) to judge the success of their team, with the result that problems tend to exist for a while before they are caught, much less corrected.

For example, a salesperson who isn't prospecting, but is good at looking busy, will have at least one month, if not an entire quarter, of not doing a behavior before being either put on a performance improvement program or let go. Unfortunately for that salesperson's employer, the behavior vacuum will ripple through that organization's sales pipeline, and possibly its bank account, depending on the length of the company's sales cycle.

By tracking leading indicators — like the number of prospecting calls and the ratio of meetings held to meetings booked — poor performance can be caught earlier in a salesperson's tenure. Catching poor performance early gives a leader an opportunity to positively coach his employee or quickly terminate if his salesperson isn't open to performance improvement. Daily check-ins, on the other hand, would get onerous for you and your team and waste your most valuable asset, your time.

TWENTY MINUTES OR LESS

Weekly check-ins can be accomplished in one of two ways, each requiring 20 minutes or less of your time.

Check-in option A is two meetings per week. A brief, meaning five minutes or less, meeting at the beginning of your week to understand what behaviors your employee plans to do that week, and a brief, 15 minutes or less, meeting at the end of the week to review results for the week and either coach on the spot or set up a time to do an in-depth coaching session.

Check-in option B is one meeting per week, 20 minutes or less, scheduled at either the very beginning or the very end of the week, to review results from the previous week — or the current week if you have your meeting at the end of the week. Use this session to provide on-the-spot coaching and to get a sense of what your employee's forthcoming behavior goals are for the week.

Because you're checking in weekly against monthly goals, you will have a clear picture by the end of the second week of each month if your employee is on pace to hit his behavior goals.

These check-in meetings are a *non-negotiable* part of the week for you and your salespeople. Some companies who use check-in option A will have each employee email his cookbook for that week to his manager for review Monday morning, but he will still keep one face-to-face or phone check-in each week because it is much harder to hide a lack of performance on the phone or in person.

UNDERSTANDING THE CONSEQUENCE LADDER

Some of your work in helping your employees understand the consequence ladder — meaning the process of getting on, moving up, moving down, and getting off the ladder — is handled by having them create their own consequences and then getting your approval. You'll usually find that your employees, the ones you want to keep anyway, will impose harsher consequences on themselves than you would have.

The key to helping your employees understand their consequence ladder is to help them trust that you will use the consequence ladder on everyone in the same way as it was agreed to in the team meeting. Your consequence ladder has to mean something. There must be no special situations for leaders or veteran team members.

START STRONG

Implementing an accountability program is a lot like raising children. The consequences have to mean something, otherwise they aren't consequences at all.

You can either go light on discipline and consequences and then try to raise the bar later, or you can start with real discipline and consequences, which only need to be used a couple of times before your employees understand that you weren't kidding about creating a culture of accountability. What you can't (or at any rate shouldn't) do is say that there will be consequences, and then fail to follow through on your word.

It is quite likely that you will only have to use your ultimate consequence, termination, once before the rest of the team gets the message about accountability.

No manager I've ever met has a problem visualizing how to apply consequences to new team members or the members of the team who chronically underperform. What a manager usually has trouble with is imagining how to apply consequences to a veteran team member, or above average performers whose production slipped. Let's look at that situation now.

APPLYING CONSEQUENCES TO VETERANS

Diane is Tiffany's manager. Tiffany was one of Diane's first hires when she took over the sales team eight years ago. Tiffany has consistently been one of Diane's top performers, but lately her behavior has tailed off and her results have followed suit. Tiffany was already on her personal consequence ladder for failing to hit her cookbook targets, but because she didn't make her numbers Diane is bumping her up to the next rung on the consequence ladder, which is working a weekend shift answering phones in customer service.

Diane: Tiffany, thanks for coming in. I don't expect this conversation will take more than nine minutes. We're going to talk about your cookbook targets. Is there anything you wanted to cover?

Tiffany: No, but what's the big deal? I know I didn't make my behavior targets, but I'm still pretty close to my sales target for the month.

Diane: Thanks for letting me know you don't have anything else you want to cover. What do you mean by "pretty close" to your sales target?

Tiffany: Well, last time I looked I was about 80 percent to target and I have a couple of deals that should close before the end of the month.

Diane: That's good. I'm curious, Tiffany, when we put cookbooks in place six weeks ago how did we do that?

Tiffany: I put together my cookbook and you approved it.

Diane: And what else did we build together?

Tiffany: The consequences that would happen if I didn't hit the targets in my cookbook.

Diane: So given that you haven't hit your cookbook for six straight weeks, what should I do?

Tiffany: You're supposed to schedule me a shift in customer service this weekend, but I don't think it's fair that I have to work the phones. I'm the most experienced person on the team. I'm just in a little slump.

Diane: I can appreciate that, Tiffany, but if you were me and I were you, what message would you be sending to the team if you didn't schedule me for a shift on the phones?

Tiffany: I guess it would say that missing your commitments is OK and that cookbooks don't really matter.

Diane: And?

Tiffany: And that would make my job harder as manager.

Diane: Because?

Tiffany: Because I would be chasing people to hit their cookbook targets but also sending them the signal that that wasn't important.

Diane: So what do you want me to do?

Tiffany: (Sighs.) Schedule my shift for this weekend. I promise I'll hit my cookbook targets next week.

Diane: Thanks, Tiffany. One more question. How can I help you hit your cookbook targets next week so we don't have to schedule you for more shifts on the phones?

Tiffany: Well....

This exchange only works because Diane had Tiffany create her cookbook instead of imposing a cookbook on her. Notice that, in the middle of the scene Diane uses one of Sandler's most powerful reversal techniques, the "If you were me" question.

"If you were me" puts your employee in your shoes and puts you in control of the conversation. For example, if Tiffany had said, "I'd just let it slide because you're a veteran," Diane could have said, "And how would that have affected the team long-term?"

Asking your employee "if you were me" puts him in a position to put the organization before himself and gives you a sense of his ability to think like a manager.

Think back to when you were starting out your career and hearing the gossip you picked up from your colleagues in the lunch room or over coffee about who got away with what. This is a perennially popular workplace topic. If you fail to apply an even hand when it comes to consequences, your employees will use your inconsistency against you in the future. It will probably sound like this: "But you let Other Employee get away with it."

Start from Day One: Make Accountability Part of Your On-boarding Plan

To truly develop a culture of accountability in your organization, accountability must be baked into your on-boarding plan.

Reasons for not putting accountability into an on-boarding plan include:

- The new employee already has too much to learn already.
- We don't want to scare him away.
- We'll let him learn from one of the veterans.

Typically, we buy into these excuses when it comes to on-boarding, and default to the on-boarding practices with which we are most familiar. Learning from a veteran employee is usually the method of choice. This is also known as a "ride along" or a "job shadow," and it is a time-honored on-boarding practice that creates mediocre employees.

Think about it this way. With whom are you putting your new hire? A top performer? Probably not. He's too busy and/or isn't a very good teacher. Consider all of the all-star athletes who became mediocre-to-terrible coaches because they couldn't impart their innate skills to others.

So you're probably putting your new hire with a "B" performer, part of that middle 60 percent who are stuck in a nice comfort zone and are, perhaps, headed slowly towards the bottom 20 percent. The ones who have a "this too shall pass" attitude towards your accountability program.

This is not to say that your new hire can't learn *anything* from your veteran team members. That learning should be very specific, though, and it should be managed in a controlled environment where you can quickly make any necessary corrections.

Let's be honest with ourselves. If a new hire makes it all the way through your sophisticated hiring process, then gets "scared away" by your accountability program, you probably don't want that person in your organization anyway!

Now, if *you* didn't *tell* your prospective hire about your accountability program during your hiring process, and you spring it on the person on the first day of work, guess whose problem that is? Yours!

Yes. A new hire has lots to learn. That doesn't mean, though, that new employees are free from accountability for their first few months on the job. Their accountability just changes a little over time. So instead of dropping your new hire head first into your accountability program, ease the person into the pool.

Effective on-boarding accountability programs have two key components. First, they exist for a defined period of time. I suggest 4-12 weeks. Second, every Friday you will test your new hire on a specific, demonstrable behavior for that week in his on-boarding accountability program.

Even though your new hire will contribute to the organization before his 12-week on-boarding program is up, we recommend that your regular accountability program doesn't kick in until after the employee completes the on-boarding accountability plan. This will help you to guard against burnout and keep employees from taking short cuts to hitting their cookbook targets. Below, you will find, as a point of reference, a sample on-boarding accountability plan I developed for one of my clients.

SAMPLE ON-BOARDING ACCOUNTABILITY PLAN FOR OUTSIDE SALESPERSON

- Deliver 30-second commercial in a networking or "introduce yourself" setting to manager.

- Deliver 30-second commercial on a prospecting call to his manager/create cookbook for approval.
- Role-play a "no pressure" prospecting call to his manager/ start cookbook behaviors.
- Set an up-front contract for a first appointment with a prospect (role-play with manager).
- Role-play uncovering compelling reasons to do business (role-play with manager).

Exercise – Your On-boarding Accountability Plan

Write down the title of a position you plan to hire for in the next 18 months _____.

Write down 4-12 specific, demonstrable behaviors you can test your new hire on in his first 4-12 weeks with your company. Each behavior should build on the last.

1. _____

_____

2. _____

_____

3. _____

_____

4. _____

_____

5. _____

_____

6. _____

_____

7. _____

_____

8. _____

_____

9. _____

_____

10. _____

_____

11. _____

_____

12. _____

_____

FIVE STEPS FOR SUCCESSFUL ACCOUNTABILITY IMPLEMENTATION

Implementing an accountability program doesn't happen over lunch.

To successfully implement an accountability program, you must commit to following these six steps:

1. Define the purpose of the program for yourself — i.e. what's the "why" of your accountability program, and do *you* believe in that purpose? By now, you should have com-

pleted an exercise on this. If you don't address this first step, your body language and tonality when you implement your program will subtly tell your employees, "This is for you, but not for me." Again: The lead dog sets the pace.

2. Start your own personal accountability program at least two weeks prior to rolling out the program for your team.

   a. If you have one or more layers of management between you and your frontline employees, create accountability programs with your direct reports and run those programs for one month before moving forward with the rest of the team.

   b. If all of the employees in your organization report directly to you, add two weeks to your personal accountability program to get even more clarity on the changes you've committed to making in your own life.

3. Preview the accountability program with select employees who either need more time to adjust to change, or who are potential champions for you when the full program rolls out. During your preview, make sure you ask your employees how they *feel* about your proposed accountability program. Get a sense of the potential roadblocks you will hit when you roll out the full program. Use the word "feel." Asking how your employees feel about your accountability program will give you better information instead of asking what they "think" of the program. You will tap into their emotions instead of just their intellect.

4. Hold an all-staff meeting to announce your accountability program and set an up-front contract with your employees around implementing cookbooks and consequences.

5. Schedule the cookbook and consequence creation meetings within the week. Do this to reduce the impression that

accountability is a "flavor of the month" program. Unless it is absolutely necessary to do so, don't let a weekend fall between step five and step six. Weekends are when anti-accountability employees will make time to develop their arguments against accountability and solidify their defenses.

Exercise – Your Implementation Deadlines

Based on the six-step implementation program above, write down the dates on which you will start each step.

1. _____

2. _____

3. _____

4. _____

5. _____

6. _____

IMPLEMENTATION FOR ONE

When you are implementing an accountability program and you are the only person on the team, your biggest asset is going to be a friend or mentor who agrees to be a second set of eyes for you. Give that person permission to make suggestions and challenge you on your plan.

Your biggest challenge in implementing your accountability program will be walking the line between the "cold turkey" and "set the bar low" camps mentioned earlier in this chapter.

I suggest that your personal accountability program be graduated just like an on-boarding accountability program, so that each week your accountabilities increase, as do the consequences for not hitting your cookbook targets. The length of your program will depend on the amount of change you plan to make. Give permission to your friend or mentor to suggest shortening or lengthening your ramp-up period if your partner feels you are being too hard or easy on yourself.

Exercise – Who Will Be Your Second Set of Eyes?

Write down the names of two people who you will ask to be your "second set of eyes" on your accountability plan. The first name is your first choice, and the second name is the person you will ask if your first choice can't or won't help.

1. _____

2. _____

THIS CHAPTER IN 45 SECONDS

- Accountability starts with you.
- Discipline means keeping appointments to yourself. Often the first person we start failing on when it comes to accountability is ourselves.
- Without discipline there can be no accountability. Without accountability there can be no discipline. Without consequences there can be neither.
- When most people make changes they either try to go cold turkey, expecting sudden change in the short-term, or they set the bar so low that no real change happens.
- Make a small change, do that for two weeks, and then evaluate and adjust your change upward.
- Sandler Rule: "No mind reading." It is our responsibility as leaders to provide clarity on our accountability program

and to test our assumptions about our employees' understanding of the program.

- There must be mutual agreement for an up-front contract to exist.

- Before you start an accountability program, you must have a clear written purpose for the program into which you buy.

- You reserve the right to suggest changes to an employee's cookbook, but you don't have the right to rip apart his initial draft.

- Set goals monthly, and manage weekly, with one or two check-in meetings per week.

- Your consequence ladder has to mean something. No special situations for leaders or veteran team members.

- Create an on-boarding accountability program of 4-12 weeks to lower the time to self-sufficiency for your new hire, and help the new hire understand your culture of accountability.

- Give select employees a preview of your accountability program before launch; ask them how they *feel* about it. Get a sense of challenges you might face when implementing the program for the entire organization.

- Move quickly to create cookbooks and consequence ladders after announcing your accountability program. Reduce the time anti-accountability employees have to hamper implementation.

CHAPTER SIX

Common Implementation Challenges and How to Fix Them

Congratulations! If you've done everything this book has set out thus far, you have successfully implemented an accountability program. And by the way, if you haven't done everything this book has set out, please put this chapter aside until you have.

Just like learning to play an instrument, speak a new language, or cook a new dish, the act of getting started is hardly the whole picture when it comes to accountability. You are likely to face challenges in the early stages of your program. There are four common implementation challenges. This chapter shows you how to handle each.

The most common implementation challenges that crop up once you have implemented your accountability program are: not being accountable; not being prepared for turnover; creative avoidance; and mutual mystification. Let's look at how these challenges are likely to appear ... and how to overcome them.

NOT BEING ACCOUNTABLE

Adults learn by observing and doing. If your employees observe you not being accountable to your cookbook, then they will do as they see and not as you say. This is why not being accountable heads our list of implementation challenges.

Most leaders aren't accountable for one of three reasons. They feel they don't need accountability, they are afraid of failure, or they don't want to be vulnerable.

"I DON'T NEED ACCOUNTABILITY"

Leaders who believe that they don't need accountability look like high achievers on the surface. They are paddling furiously below, though, just to keep their head above water.

Even so, a leader with a "no accountability for me" mindset may attempt to implement an accountability program for the others in the organization. After all, everyone else *does* need to be held accountable! Otherwise, the leader believes, people would continue to sit around doing nothing, while the leader huffs and puffs and keeps the organization running. (You may have worked in an organization with a leader like this at some point in your career.)

Leaders who stay in this mindset will realize a lot of personal frustration, reduced morale, and increased turnover as they attempt to lead from the rear, but they will not be able to implement a successful accountability program. That's a promise.

If you have friends who feel they don't need accountability, but who feel that their team does, you might suggest they complete the following exercise.

Exercise – I Don't Need Accountability Because...

1. Complete this sentence: "I don't need accountability because...":

_____

_____

_____

2. Why are you sure that the sentence you just wrote is true? What evidence do you have to support it?

_____

_____

_____

3. Let's pretend, only for the sake of argument, that your response to #1 above *isn't* true. How would that affect your organization?

_____

_____

_____

4. Based on your answer to #4, above, how would you, personally, be different?

_____

_____

_____

BEING AFRAID OF FAILURE

For leaders, especially high-performing leaders, fear of failure is totally normal. For many of us it's a script we carry from our parents. "It's OK if you don't get an 'A,' Cindy, just don't fail." We hear that kind of thing at an impressionable age, and we may hear it over and over. Perhaps mom and dad were trying to be encouraging, but they weren't helping us prepare for success after grade school. One of David Sandler's rules goes as follows: "You have to learn to fail to win." As we grow in our careers, though, many of us take most of our lessons from our successes and ignore the failures. That sometimes makes things difficult

Look at this exchange between Dave, the owner of a midsized manufacturer of doors, who wants to implement an accountability program within his company, and Phil, his coach:

Phil: Thanks for inviting me in, Dave. What did you want to discuss today?

Dave: Phil, I want to implement an accountability program for my organization. I believe that we're doing well, but we aren't as effective as we could be. I did some quick calculations and it looks like we could increase our net profit by six to eight percent annually if everyone knew the specific tasks expected of them each month and the consequences for not performing.

Phil: Sounds like you've got the bones of a good idea here, Dave. Not sure where I can help...

Dave: Well, part of an accountability program would be that I would be part of the program with my own personal behavior plan and consequences.

Phil: And?

Dave: And I feel like I have to hold myself to some unimpeachable standard to do that.

Phil: Because?

Dave: Because if I don't hit the targets I committed to, which I designed myself, why would my employees want to work for me?

Phil: I see. Dave, may I ask you a tough question?

Dave: Um, I guess.

Phil: Am I perfect?

Dave: What?

Phil: Am I perfect, Dave?

Dave: Well, no. Nobody's perfect.

Phil: What do you mean?

Dave: Well, you're not perfect. I'm certainly not perfect. I don't have any perfect employees. One or two think they are.

Phil: So?

Dave: So if no one is perfect then I shouldn't stress myself out over being perfect.

Phil: That makes sense. What are you going to do now?

Dave: Get this accountability plan off my desk and implement it for myself tomorrow. I want to play with it for a couple weeks first and then roll it out to the team.

Phil: Sounds like you've got another good plan in your hands, Dave. Let me know how I can help.

Dave: I will, Phil. I'm excited to get going with my accountability plan.

BEING AFRAID TO BE VULNERABLE

Go ask 10, 1,000, or 10,000 people what the first word they think of is when they hear the word "vulnerable" and you're likely to get some version of the word "weak."

Enlightened leaders understand that being vulnerable is one of the strongest positions you can take ... assuming that your goal as a leader is to be loved instead of feared.

In the context of accountability, the feedback we've had from leaders about fear of vulnerability ranges from "I can't share that (my cookbook) with my team," to "You've got to be kidding me. Post my goals on the intranet?" to "How is this going to help me?"

Our resistance to being vulnerable relates directly to our "fight or flight" response, which is coded into our limbic brain. To be vulnerable means putting yourself in a position where you are likely to be injured, and that is something our brain is coded to resist.

These days, most of the "injuries" we get as leaders are psychological or emotional, but our brain hasn't evolved enough to recognize that exposing your goals to your team, which could (it seems to some) result in mockery, isn't the same as facing down a charging bear with nothing but your fists and your feet for defense.

Yet sharing goals creates a kind of vulnerability that is, for most leaders, not dangerous at all. Unless your organization is strictly command and control, and I mean an organization that is quasi-military in nature, sharing your goals with your team humanizes you and creates a culture of trust.

Exercise – Why Are You Afraid?

Write down all of the fears you have about implementing an accountability program, especially those that relate to failing at your own accountability or being vulnerable to your team.

For each fear you wrote down above, write down the positive benefit to you and your company if that fear was unfounded.

NOT BEING PREPARED FOR TURNOVER

Implementing accountability means you will experience turnover in your organization. Period. If the thought of losing even one (probably low-performing) employee is paralyzing, *stop reading right now and give the book to someone who lives in the real world!*

I worked with a manufacturer's representative that, in the first 12 months of implementing an accountability program, had 100 percent turnover in his organization. Everyone, aside from the owners, left. Now this company only had 10 employees, but the owners of the company speak proudly of the turnover they experienced because through their accountability program they were able to quantify their gut feelings that they had the wrong people working for them. And they did. Fortunately, most of the turnover came from employees who self-selected by deciding to leave the company. They could see that they could no longer get away with their unproductive behaviors.

Exercise – Your New Bus

You have a bus that has two less seats than the number of people on your team. So if you have a team of four, including you, there are two seats on the bus because you're the driver. Write down the names of the two people who don't make it onto your new bus.

_____

_____

_____

In round numbers, how much in base salary alone would you save if those two people weren't on your bus?

_____

If those two people wouldn't be on your new bus, why are they on your current bus?

_____

_____

_____

_____

_____

_____

_____

_____

Being prepared for turnover doesn't mean that you hired bad people. It means that each of your employees has his own motivation for working for your company — you'll recall that we covered those motivations in the "Start with the Mountaintop" chapter — and accountability might not fit into that motivation.

By now, you should have a good picture of which members of your team will be likely to self-select shortly after you launch your accountability program. This is only natural, and it's one of the reasons you as a leader must always be recruiting.

Members of the Sandler Management Solutions program know that, as leaders, they need to recruit constantly. Recruiting must be part of your accountability implementation strategy, otherwise you will fall prey to desperation recruiting, which typically results in hiring someone who simply "looks good" for a role, instead of being the right fit for that role.

Remember, being prepared for turnover does not mean that you hired bad fits or that the individuals who resign are bad people. Turnover is part of any organization, and managed turnover is part of any successful organization. In a perfect world, you would start your recruiting efforts six to eight weeks in advance so that your pool of qualified replacements is ready to go should you need them. Not everyone is in a position to work that far in advance, however. Regardless of your organization's timeline, you should ramp up your recruiting efforts as part of your accountability campaign.

CREATIVE AVOIDANCE

Creative avoidance simply means not being accountable to perform the right behaviors. Sometimes, accountability programs go off track because they don't focus on the right stuff! When implementing an accountability program ask yourself, "Does X advance my business?" (X being the activities to which you will hold yourself or your people accountable.)

Let's take a look at several examples that will illustrate how this self-questioning process works.

- Activity – understanding your direct reports' personal goals.
  - **Does it advance my business?** Absolutely. Leaders who understand the personal goals of their direct reports can tie the achievement of corporate goals to each direct report achieving his personal goals — which typically results in more motivated and productive employees.
- Activity – going on sales calls as the "closer."
  - **Does it advance my business?** No. Having the boss in a meeting may impress a prospect, but being brought in as the "closer" stunts your salespeople's growth and becomes a time deficit for you.
- Activity – giving your employees the answer when coaching.
  - **Does it advance my business?** Not really. Telling someone what to do or giving him the answer to his problem is called "tactical" coaching. It's OK to coach tactically on occasion, but it is better to coach *strategically,* which not only helps your employee address his own problem, but also stops the problem from happening again.
- Activity – holding your salespeople accountable to their weekly prospecting plan.
  - **Does it advance my business?** Yes. Holding each salesperson accountable to his weekly prospecting plan (number of calls, meetings, networking events, referral requests, etc.) should take as little as 20 minutes per week: 5 minutes on Monday and 15 minutes on Friday. By holding twice-weekly accountability meetings, you eliminate any mystification about what your salespeople are doing to grow your business and

have an early warning system to detect problems before the end of a quarter.

One of the most common implementation challenges is holding employees accountable to activities which appear to advance your business, but are actually detrimental in the long-term or (just as bad) are results, and not activities at all.

Case in Point – Rewarding Behaviors That Are Detrimental in the Long-Term

A cable television company implemented a compensation program that gave a bonus for each new customer activation, regardless of credit rating or type of package purchased. Naturally, the number of new subscribers skyrocketed in the first 30 days of the program, and then dove sharply as soon as the new customers received their first bill. The program was swiftly abandoned.

Salespeople are slaves to their compensation program. Human beings are slaves to our brain's reward systems, even if the behavior being rewarded is detrimental in the long-term. For example, if you eat a donut today, you get a reward from your brain, which likes sugar, and you won't notice any immediate detrimental effects to your appearance or physical health (unless, of course, you drip jelly on your shirt). However, pounding back a half-dozen donuts a day over time will, eventually, result in negative effects.

Similarly, holding your employees accountable to targets like "number of customer service calls answered per hour," "number of widgets produced per day," or "number of videos produced per week" may initially give you good outputs ... but the targets are superficial. Eventually your employees will burn out and customers will turn away from the poor products and/or poor service.

You do not want to reward actions that don't lead to results. For example, holding your salespeople accountable to a certain number of cold calls or networking events each week makes sense *if there is an expected result* (e.g., X number of unique conversations) attached to the target. It is possible to make hundreds of horrible cold calls to the same dozen or so people, or to turn networking events into a waste of time. If the behaviors in your accountability program put your salespeople on a hamster wheel instead of on a path to a mountaintop, you must adjust their behaviors accordingly.

Accountability is a long-term strategy, not a Band-Aid. When deciding on behaviors to hold your employees accountable to, translate the desired outcome (for instance, "increased customer satisfaction with customer service calls") into a small, measurable behavior for your employees (for instance, "ask at the end of each call how satisfied your customer is with the call on a scale of 1-10"). Because you already track how many calls each customer service representative answers each day, you can see from his cookbook whether he asked that question on each call. If he is asking that question, then your desired outcome should follow. If he isn't asking, then you have a coaching opportunity to find out why and fix the underlying cause of his task avoidance.

BEHAVIOR OR RESULT?

In our experience one of the biggest problems with traditional management is holding direct reports responsible for a result (for instance, a closed sale) instead of the behaviors that lead to the result (for instance, prospecting and qualifying).

This is where having a defined process with specific, measurable behaviors at each step of the process is critical. If you run into this problem, it's almost certainly because there is a lack of clarity about your process.

Let's use sales as an example. If your organization doesn't have a clearly defined sales process — not a sales methodology, but a unique process for selling that is distinct to your organization — that is written out and clearly understood by everyone on your sales team, if not your entire organization, then implementing an accountability program with the sales team will be almost impossible. Why? Because you have to hold each individual salesperson accountable to the organization's process. There can be, and should be, personalized cookbooks — but the larger sales process must *not* be personalized!

Case in Point – Sales Process

Below is an example of a four-step sales process for a simple software sale. Included are the time between steps, the specific behaviors expected in each step, and the result expected at the end of each step.

1. Prospecting – time between conversation with prospect and discovery meeting, 1-2 weeks
   A. Expected behaviors
      a. Prospecting calls
      b. Networking
      c. Referral requests
      d. LinkedIn® prospecting
      e. Responding to inbound requests
   B. Result expected: unique conversation with decision maker.
   C. Next step: close file and move on to other prospects or book discovery meeting.
2. Discovery meeting – time between discovery meeting and second meeting, 1-4 weeks

A. Expected behaviors:
   a. Set up-front contract at beginning and end of meeting
   b. Pre-meeting plan
   c. Post-meeting debrief
   d. Uncover prospect's compelling reasons for doing business with us versus competitor
   e. Uncover prospect's decision-making process including everyone who will be involved and their role
   f. Obtain information about prospect's budget including how he would make an investment in our product
B. Result expected: closed file or next meeting confirmed with prospect with up-front contract for all decision makers to be present and a clear "no" or "yes" decision made at the end of the meeting.
C. Next step:
   a. If file is closed, get permission to add prospect to drip marketing campaign and/or set a clear future to reconnect.
   b. If meeting is booked, confirm there are no reasons why the meeting would be moved or cancelled.

3. Second meeting/demo – time between second meeting and implementation, 1-4 weeks
   A. Expected behaviors:
      a. Set up-front contract at beginning and end of meeting
      b. Pre-meeting plan
      c. Post-meeting debrief

    d. Reconfirm information obtained in discovery meeting relating to prospect's compelling reasons to do business, budget and decision-making process

    e. Confirm nothing has changed with the prospect's situation since the discovery meeting

    f. Demo product per prospect's direction

    g. Confirm sale

    h. Sign paperwork

    i. Address buyer's remorse

    j. Open discussion about future business and/or referrals/testimonials

B. Result expected: closed file or confirmed sale with implementation date.

C. Next step:

    a. If file is closed, get permission to add prospect to drip marketing campaign and/or set a clear future to reconnect.

    b. If sale is closed, confirm there are no reasons why the sale would be delayed or cancelled.

4. Implementation/close: implement software per previously signed paperwork and agree to communication method and frequency.

Represented graphically, that process looks like this:

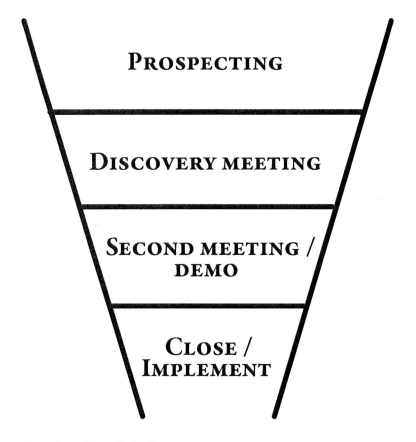

Exercise – Your Sales Process

Write down the steps in your organization's sales process. For each step, include the time between steps, the specific behaviors expected in each step, and the result expected at the end of each step.

_____

_____

_____

_____

_____

_____

_____

Defining your sales process allows you to take control of your sales cycle and hold your salespeople accountable to specific, measurable behaviors that advance your business.

Once that you have a defined sales process published where anyone in your organization can see it, you can coach salespeople who are struggling to create better accountability plans and beneficial behaviors to include in their cookbooks.

Without real data to analyze about specific behaviors, enacting change is extremely difficult!

One of the biggest misconceptions about accountability programs is that they are time sinks (see chapter two). In reality, no one is so busy that he can't make a mark on a piece of paper or change a "one" to a "two" on a spreadsheet during his day. At the beginning of an accountability program, the act of recording your behaviors may seem daunting, but as you maintain your discipline to your cookbook, the time spent on recording and analyzing your numbers will become more manageable, part of your everyday routine. You may even come to consider the time you spend with your cookbook to be a welcome respite from the other demands on your time.

The other departments in your company probably have processes written down to accomplish the results required of them, so, for those departments, breaking down their process into specific, measurable behaviors should be much easier than for your sales team.

Getting all of your company's processes written down and broken into specific, measurable behaviors may sound like a lot of work up front. Consider what happens, though, when an organization loses that veteran employee who "had it all in his head." Those organizations then have to either go through the pain of figuring out what that employee knew from any random notes left behind, or from stories colleagues have about working with that employee — or they have to bring back that employee as a consultant at additional expense to the company.

By getting all of your processes written down you protect institutional knowledge and decrease time to self-sufficiency during on-boarding. New hires don't have to waste time collecting fragments of information from various people in the department.

Processes should give employees flexibility to put their personality into applying the process while still staying within the boundaries of the process. For example, if step three of your sales process is to do a demo, the way your salesperson gets to step three is by completing steps one and two; however, how the salesperson goes about completing steps one and two will be based on the salesperson's (and the prospect's) personality and preferred communication style.

If you hear that your employees feel restricted by certain parts of your process, take time to examine whether the process allows them to be flexible while staying within the boundaries of the process. Few people like to be told exactly what to do and when to do it, but most people are OK with staying within the boundaries of a well-designed process.

Exercise – Institutional Knowledge

Write down the names of all the employees in your organization who possess a critical piece of institutional knowledge that is not yet written down. Write down the date by which you will ask them to write down that knowledge.

_____

_____

_____

_____

_____

_____

_____

_____

_____

_____

MUTUAL MYSTIFICATION

Mutual mystification happens when one party in a conversation doesn't verify that the message sent to the other party is the message that was received.

When implementing an accountability program, mutual mystification usually manifests when employees do not create personal accountability plans because they aren't sure of the purpose of the program, or when employees avoid their weekly commitments because they believe the purpose of the accountability program is "gotcha" management.

In both cases, the problem lies in a poor up-front contract when your accountability program was announced. By this point, you should know how to fix this.

MISUNDERSTANDING THE PURPOSE OF YOUR ACCOUNTABILITY PROGRAM

Misunderstanding the purpose of your accountability program comes from a lack of clarity about your purpose for implementing accountability in your organization.

Let's face it: Implementing an accountability program requires a lot of work from both you and your employees. A lack of clarity in purpose will kill your accountability program before it has a chance to take root. It's worth taking a few moments to troubleshoot the "why" of your accountability program.

Exercise – Revisit the Purpose of Your Accountability Program

Revisit what you wrote down in the previous chapter about the purpose (the "why") of your accountability. Identify at least three places where mutual mystification could develop.

Now rewrite the purpose for your accountability program to eliminate potential mutual mystification.

_____

_____

_____

_____

_____

_____

_____

_____

_____

_____

_____

Your purpose, like an up-front contract, must be clearly stated and explicit in its terms.

TASK AVOIDANCE FROM EMPLOYEES

When employees engage in task avoidance, one, or a combination, of the following three issues are at work.

- The organization's culture is highly politicized.
- Their cookbooks were given to them instead of created by them.
- They aren't on board with your consequence ladder.

Implementing an accountability program requires trust and vulnerability from everyone in the organization, including senior management. In a highly politicized culture neither trust nor vulnerability abound.

If you are a leader who has inherited a highly politicized culture or team, we suggest taking a step back from implementing the accountability program and first uncover the reasons behind the politicization of your team. Then break down the barriers of communication affecting the next level of leaders, and so on, until you've broken down communication barriers affecting frontline employees. Children learn how to behave by watching the adults in their lives; similarly, employees learn by observing the behavior of their peers and managers, and by noticing the rewards or punishments that that behavior receives. You must change this underlying dynamic, not just the words that are spoken in the organization. Here are two ways to do that.

First, change your own observable daily routine. Consider a task that your current managers see as menial, emptying the break room dishwasher for example, and start doing that task regularly. What you should notice, in a few weeks, is other members of your team emptying the dishwasher or performing other tasks that they might have passed by previously. This action will also help you identify the individuals on your team who *aren't* suited to continue with you, as they will either complain loudly about your actions ("Why are you doing that? We have 'people' to do that.") or avoid pitching in. The latter action will eventually separate and isolate them from the rest of the team, possibly causing them to move on to another professional opportunity, or, at the very least, making it easier for you to remove them when you move back to full implementation of accountability program.

Second, be more explicit with the team about your accountability program for yourself. As you model behavior for your team, begin sharing more of your personal accountability story so your team sees that trust and vulnerability are actually beneficial to the success of the organization.

Exercise – "Menial" Tasks

Write down one or two "menial" tasks, like emptying the break room dishwasher, that you will start doing and a date within the next week when you will do that task for the first time.

AVOIDING THE COOKBOOK

When employees are avoiding their cookbooks, this typically means that management had too much influence in the activities (behaviors) required in each employee's cookbook.

Yes, the up-front contract for implementing an accountability program includes your right as leader to approve or suggest changes to an employee's cookbook and require certain behaviors to be included. However, the reason(s) for the required behaviors must be explicitly and clearly stated by you and understood by your employee. If your employees don't understand *why* a particular behavior is required in their cookbook, they will avoid doing that behavior.

Exercise – Required Tasks and Reasons

Write down a role and a department in your organization (e.g., Marketing Assistant, Marketing) and the two to four combined "non-negotiable" and "need-to-have" behaviors you expect in that cookbook.

Role _____

Department _____

_____

_____

_____

_____

_____

_____

_____

_____

Now write down *a reason* for each of those behaviors that's explicitly and clearly stated so there is no mutual mystification about why your employee will include those behaviors in his cookbook.

_____

_____

_____

_____

_____

_____

_____

_____

_____

_____

AVOIDING THE CONSEQUENCE LADDER

When employees aren't onboard with your consequence ladder, this usually means there was too much management say in the types of consequences or the way an employee would get on, move up and down, or step off the consequence ladder. It is likely there is too little trust between management and employees.

In organizations with low trust, employees will regard a consequence ladder as yet another stick for management to beat them with or hold over their heads. In organizations with high trust, employees will regard a consequence ladder as the natural result of failing to hold themselves accountable to the behaviors they set for themselves.

Getting employees on board with their consequence ladders typically requires an open, honest conversation about the reasons for having consequences in an accountability program. You must ensure that each employee understands that this is not a trick, but a tool meant to help the team, including this employee, achieve at the highest level. You do not intend to fire the person. If you wanted to fire the person, he or she would be gone already!

IMPLEMENTATION PROBLEMS FOR ONE

When implementing an accountability program for one, the two most common implementation challenges you will face are procrastination and maintaining momentum beyond the first few weeks of your program.

David Sandler said, "A decision not to make a decision is a decision." Deciding to implement an accountability program, but not deciding on an implementation date, means not deciding to implement an accountability program! Create a significant financial or time consequence if you fail to take action on your personal accountability program. Commit to that significant financial or time consequence in writing. Recruit a friend to help hold you to this consequence. This could be committing to donate a large amount of money to your favorite charity or, possibly more motivating, an anti-charity — that is, a cause you *don't* support. This could also be committing to a large number of volunteer hours for a local non-profit. Whatever consequence you choose, it must be significant enough to motivate you to avoid it

The other big challenge has to do with momentum. Perhaps two to three weeks into your new program, you start to lose momentum and motivation to keep going. You begin to feel like you are running in place with your cookbook. It's around this time that your excuse generator kicks in.

The excuse generator is wonderful at creating seemingly legitimate reasons to avoid doing the behaviors in your cookbook. The best way to defeat the excuse generator is to *write down* whatever excuse it throws your way. Once the excuse is out of your head and onto a piece of paper or computer screen, you can eliminate it rationally.

Once you turn off your excuse generator, build small rewards into hitting your cookbook goals. Human beings tend to repeat behavior that is rewarded, whether it is beneficial or detrimental. By rewarding yourself for hitting your cookbook targets from week one, you will train your brain to shut down your excuse generator and drive you to reach your targets each week so you get your reward.

Exercise – Excuse Generator and Rewards

Write down the excuses your excuse generator will produce to knock you off your cookbook. For instance: "I'm too tired to make calls." Next to each write down a response to eliminate that excuse. For instance: "Not as tired as I'll be if I have to work late catching up on my cookbook targets."

_____

_____

_____

_____

_____

_____

_____

_____

_____

Write down a small reward you will give yourself each week for hitting your cookbook targets. The reward can change, but it should be small.

_____

_____

_____

_____

_____

_____

_____

_____

This Chapter in 45 Seconds

- Most leaders aren't accountable because they feel they don't need accountability, they are afraid of failure, or they don't want to be vulnerable.

- Attempting to implement accountability in your organization without being accountable yourself will result in a lot of personal frustration, reduced morale, and unacceptable turnover levels.

- Fear of failure is totally normal. For many of us, it's a script we carry from our parents.

- David Sandler's first rule was, "You have to learn to fail to win."

- Enlightened leaders understand that being vulnerable is one of the strongest positions you can take if your goal as a leader is to be loved instead of feared.

- Implementing accountability means you will experience some turnover in your organization.

- Leaders need to Always Be Recruiting (ABR).

- A successful recruiting strategy starts by clearly creating a job profile for the role.

- When implementing an accountability program ask yourself, "Does X advance my business?" (X being the activities to which you will hold yourself or your people accountable).

- Human beings are slaves to the brain's reward systems, even if the behavior being rewarded is detrimental in the long-term.

- Never manage the numbers (results) — manage the behavior.

- Have each of your departments write down the processes they use to achieve their results, and then break those processes into specific, measureable behaviors.

- Mutual mystification happens when one party in a conversation doesn't verify that the message sent to the other party is the message that was received.

- People misunderstanding the purpose of your accountability program comes from a lack of clarity in your "why" behind implementing accountability in your organization.

- Implementing an accountability program requires trust and vulnerability from everyone in the organization, including senior management.

- When employees are avoiding their cookbooks, this typically means that management had too much influence in the activities (behaviors) required in each employee's cookbook.

- When the consequence ladder system is implemented correctly, employees create and use their own consequence ladder.

- Individuals who implement accountability programs typically have problems with either procrastination or keeping momentum going after the first two to three weeks of starting their program. To counter this, create more meaningful consequences, use the excuse generator, and create a system of small rewards.

EPILOGUE

Thank you for taking the first step on your accountability journey.

From chapter one you have an idea of what causes the "Big Brother," "Too Much Time," "Veteran Team," and "They'll Leave" myths about accountability and some tools to help you conquer the myth(s) that hold you back from implementing an accountability program.

From chapter two you understand that accountability starts by defining your mountaintops and helping your team define theirs. You will also recognize the difference between goals and quotas and why the former is a greater motivator than the latter.

From chapter three you know how to use a cookbook to design a path to reach any mountaintop, and why managing by leading indicators is your surest way to correcting poor performance and helping your team grow.

From chapter four you understand that without consequences there can be no accountability, but consequences can be both negative and positive. You also have strategies and tactics for having a consequences conversation with your team.

From chapter five you have a path for implementing an accountability program, which starts with you being a model for your team.

From chapter six you are aware of the most common challenges that arise when implementing an accountability program and how to overcome them with your program intact.

This book is the result of many collaborative experiences with my clients. I hope you will continue the collaboration by helping me make this content better. I look forward to continuing the accountability discussion with you!

To your continued success,

Hamish Knox
Sandler Training

CONGRATULATIONS!

Accountability
The Sandler Way

includes a complimentary seminar!

Take this opportunity to personally experience the non-traditional sales training and reinforcement coaching that has been recognized internationally for decades.

Companies in the Fortune 1000 as well as thousands of small- to medium-sized businesses choose Sandler Training for sales, leadership, management, and a wealth of other skill-building programs. Now, it's your turn, and it's free!

You'll learn the latest practical, tactical, feet-in-the-street sales methods directly from your neighborhood Sandler trainers! They're knowledgeable, friendly, and informed about your local selling environment.

Here's how you redeem YOUR FREE SEMINAR invitation.

1. Go to www.Sandler.com and click on the LOCATE A TRAINING CENTER button (upper right corner).
2. Select your location from the drop-down menus.
3. Review the list of all the Sandler trainers in your area.
4. Call your local Sandler trainer, mention *Accountability The Sandler Way,* and reserve your place at the next seminar!